D0903814

PIERRE TEILHARD DE CHARDIN

Pierre Teilhard de Chardin

PIERRE

# TEILHARD DE CHARDIN

*His Life and Spirit*

*By*

NICOLAS CORTE 



TRANSLATED BY

MARTIN JARRETT-KERR, C. R.

New York
THE MACMILLAN COMPANY
1961

from the original French edition
*La vie et l'âme de Teilhard de Chardin*


Second Printing 1961

Printed in the United States of America

Library of Congress catalog card number: 60-12446

## CONTENTS

# PREFACE TO THE ENGLISH EDITION

THE two books that have moved me most in the last decade have both been French. Simone Weil's *L'Attente de Dieu* ('Waiting on God') revealed a spiritual search of such intensity that as I read it I had to get up several times from my chair and walk about the room. Yet what I now remember of it is precisely the intensity of that search rather than anything she believed or taught. When, however, nearly two years ago I read Père Teilhard de Chardin's *Le Phénomène humain* ('The Phenomenon of Man'), there was certainly an intense human experience in the book (though I knew nothing, at the time, about the man), but there was also much more: there was that new way of looking at existence which results in a slight but permanent shift in one's attitude to everything. Such books occur (perhaps mercifully) only once or twice in a lifetime: but they are such that after reading them it is almost impossible to remember what things looked like before, except that they *all* looked different.

*

In this Introduction of M. Corte's book to English readers I shall try to do two things. I shall fill in some of the gaps in this necessarily brief study—for more material, more memoirs and letters have appeared since M. Corte wrote. And I shall try to suggest something of Père Teilhard's importance in the English philosophical-theological scene.

I

One of the most charming tributes to Père Teilhard comes from his agnostic Chinese scientific colleague, Chung-Chien Young:

> 'Although he was a Catholic he had, to my great astonishment, an exceptionally wide knowledge of the natural sciences. He had come to China as a result of a sort of punishment imposed upon

him by the Cardinal for something he had written against the idea of religion.[1]

The naïve incomprehension of this is as affecting as its sincerity. Teilhard had not, of course, been 'punished' by any 'Cardinal', and he had not 'written against the idea of religion'. It is true that his Order (the Jesuits) in France had become anxious about the trend of his scientific-philosophical thought, not merely because it openly championed Evolution but because it seemed to leave no room for 'special creation' or for divine Grace; so that they were relieved to have him well out of the way, in China. And this anxiety grew rather than diminished as time went on, leading to the refusal of an *imprimatur* for any of his books. More, he was not allowed to let his name go forward as a candidate for a Professorship in the Collège de France (one of the highest honours in that country: as a sort of reprisal for this refusal he was elected a Member of the Institut (1950), as he had previously, in 1947, been made an officer of the Légion d'honneur). He was not allowed, from 1947 till the day of his death, to give public lectures in France; and in 1954 was forbidden to travel from New York to attend an international palaeontological congress in Paris, called by his friend Jean Piveteau—he had to content himself with sending a communication. What is remarkable in all this—and M. Corte hardly does justice to it—is Teilhard's astonishing loyalty not only to the Church but to his Order. Hardly a murmur can be detected in any of his letters, and though he once does say to a priest friend in 1953 'Pray hard for me that I may not die bitter',[2] he never wavered. It was sometimes suggested that at least he should, like the abbé Bremond, leave the Jesuits and become a secular priest, which would have given him slightly greater freedom: but he replied that that would not only deny his vocation but undermine the very ideas of Christian community which it was part of his evolutionary message to commend. In 1948 he visited Rome, to try to obtain the *imprimatur* for *Le Phénomène humain* and leave to stand as a Candidate for the Collège de France. While there he was introduced to the formidable Père Garrigou-Lagrange, the great Dominican theologian and a powerful influence against him; Teilhard writes that 'we smiled at each other and talked about the Auvergne'.[3] Of course neither permission was granted. Indeed, before his death the Editor of *Etudes* told Teilhard confidentially that his works would never receive the *imprimatur* so that he had better take any action necessary to secure their

[1] Cit. in Claude Cuénot, *Pierre Teilhard de Chardin, les grandes Etapes de son évolution* (Plon, 1958), p. 206. [2] Cuènot, p. 447. [3] Ibid., p. 326.

posthumous publication outside the Church. Hence the distinguished committee of scientists and men of letters which sponsored these books after his death.[1]

Teilhard was certainly an unconventional figure among Jesuits. His Chinese friend and colleague, Dr. C. C. Young, tells us of a visit they paid together to the fossiliferous fissures at Wahnsien. They could not obtain accommodation for the night, so Père Teilhard suggested that they try the Catholic Mission. A Chinese priest appeared:

> 'and looked at us with a very strange expression, as if he suspected us of being criminals. He asked Père Teilhard's profession, for he was, as usual, in his geologist's rig-out. We told him the truth—that he was a Catholic priest—but of course he didn't believe it, and started to talk to Père Teilhard in Latin. Although Père Teilhard knew Latin well, he hadn't had the occasion to speak it for years. So he couldn't talk fluently with the Chinese Catholic priest, whose suspicions were thus confirmed. . . .'

They were given very poor accommodation for two days, till the priest had had time to telegraph the Central Mission—after which he moved them with apologies to better quarters.[2] On the Croisière Jaune, the Citroën expedition across Turkestan and Mongolia, on which Teilhard was official geologist, not one of the party was a practising Catholic; but on January 1st, 1932, Teilhard said a Mass before they set out, and everyone attended. One of them wrote to his wife that:

[1] Since the English edition of *The Phenomenon of Man* does not reprint this impressive list from the French, it may be of interest to give some of the better-known names: C. Arambourg (Honorary Professor of Palaeontology at the Muséum National d'Histoire Naturelle); Dr. G. B. Barbour (Professor of Geology, Dean of the Faculty of Arts and Sciences of the University of Cincinnati); A. C. Blanc (Director of the Istituto italiano di Paleontologia, Umbria); Abbé H. Breuil (Member of the Académie des Inscriptions, Honorary Professor of Prehistory at the Collège de France, Professor of Human Palaeontology); Duc M. de Broglie (Member of the Académie Française and of the Académie des Sciences); L. Fage (former President of the Académie des Sciences); Dorothy Garrod (Oxford, Fellow of British Academy); Sir Julian Huxley; G. H. R. von Koenigswald (Professor of Palaeontology at the State University of Utrecht); H. L. Movius (Peabody Museum, Harvard University); Jean Piveteau (Professor at the Sorbonne); G. G. Simpson (American Museum of Natural History, Professor of Vertebrate Paleontology, Columbia University); A. S. Romer (Professor of Zoology, Harvard University); C. van Riet Lowe (First Director, Archaeological Survey, Union of South Africa); H. V. Vallois (Director of the Musée de l'Homme, Paris); S. Westoll (Professor of Geology, Durham University). These are the scientists. Among the Men of Letters: Arnold Toynbee; R. Aron; Jacques Chevalier; G. Duhamel; Jean Hyppolite; Jean Lacroix; André Malraux; Léopold Sédar Senghor; André Siegfried; Jean Wahl.

[2] Cuénot, p. 224.

'It was a very moving sight to see all these men in their expedition-kit, gathered together in this little chapel lost in the heart of China, recollecting themselves before God prior to facing all the unforeseen that lay between them and their goal. . . .'[1]

And in his unusual sermon before this Mass, Teilhard addressed them all:

'My dear friends. Here we are this morning, all together in this little church . . . to begin this new year in the face of God. God, no doubt, has not the same precise meaning, the same face, for each of us. But because we are all men, none of us can escape the sense . . . that above us and in front of us there exists a higher energy, in which we must recognize—since it is higher—the enlarged equivalent of our own intelligence and will. It is in this powerful Presence that we should be recollected for a moment at the beginning of this year. We ask this Presence to unite us . . . with those whom we love, far away. . . . And we beg His all-powerful Presence . . . to crown our enterprise with success, and that any suffering which may befall us . . . may be transformed in the higher joy of taking our little place in the universe and having done what was our duty. It is so that this may happen that I shall offer to Him, for all of you, this Mass—the highest form of Christian prayer.'[2]

Very often he was not able to say Mass at all on his various expeditions, and then he would pray:

'Since, Lord, once again . . . in the steppes of Asia, I have neither bread nor wine nor altar, I will raise myself above these symbols up to the pure majesty of Reality, and I, your priest, will offer You, upon the altar of the whole Earth, the labour and the suffering of the world.'[3]

Yet he was strict in fulfilling his obligations as a priest. On one expedition he had an accident, and George Barbour, the American geologist, records how he had to read bits of the Breviary to him in bed.[4] And a divorced friend who consulted him about re-marriage, thinking he would take a 'liberal' view, found him intransigeant.[5] Everyone who knew him speaks of his simple faith and sanctity, and his Jesuit superiors were struck by his humility, openness and sense of complete obedience. Though he had to live in silence—indeed, his Order protected him in a

[1] Cuénot gives the facsimile of the letter, p. 154.
[2] Cuénot, p. 167.
[3] *Messe sur le Monde.*
[4] Cuénot, p. 226.
[5] Ibid., p. 139.

sense, for they knew that if his works had been published they would have been condemned—he accepted it, in the quiet and serene belief that the truth in his message would reach men eventually. As it is now doing.

II

A testy writer in *The Times Literary Supplement* (31 July 1959) recently attacked Christian apologists who:

> 'try to convince the ungodly by borrowing their own weapons of argument. This ill-advised attempt to marry absolutism with scientific method has, perhaps, done more than anything else to discredit the whole movement among serious students.'

And he goes on to give examples, among which are:

> 'Père Teilhard de Chardin's attempted reconciliation of Christianity with evolution (which, *inter alia*, predicts a *cultural* super-organism developing in a direct line from physical mutations).'

No one who had *read* Teilhard could be guilty of so monstrously misleading an account. Sir Julian Huxley, in his review-article of *Le Phénomène humain* (*Encounter*, April 1956), says that 'he often saw further and with keener vision than I ever did'. And in a Symposium at Columbia (N.Y.) on 'The Unity of Human Knowledge' in 1954, 'a profound—and vigorous cleavage appeared between humanists and scientists' on the question 'Is Man still biologically developing?' 'I naturally', says Teilhard, 'took up the position strongly (with Huxley and the great majority of scientists) against the immobilist position of—alas—the most Christianized elements in the section, namely, Gilson, Malik . . . and even Van Dusen.'[1] And it is worth noting that the theme of man's cultural development being the continuation of his evolution is argued on somewhat similar terms, though quite independently, by a geneticist who is not likely to have much sympathy for 'Christian scientific apologetics', namely Professor C. H. Waddington, in his Woodhull Lecture, 1959.[2]

No, Teilhard in all his works writes primarily as a naturalist. He is not concerned to 'reconcile' evolution with anything. 'Reconcile' begs the question: we reconcile what is separate, hostile, at odds. But Teilhard's life was spent saying that Evolution itself cannot be understood so long as 'man' is considered to be a sort of 'sport', a dead

[1] *Nouvelles Lettres de Voyage*, pp. 180 f.

[2] *Nature*, 13 June, 1959.

(because not evolving) branch sticking out sideways from the main evolutionary trunk. This is not primarily 'Christian apologetic' at all (here I disagree with M. Corte): it is simply discourse about the real. And if Teilhard did address himself to scientists—urging them to take proper account of 'man' in their science—he addressed himself more urgently to Christians, telling them what scientific discoveries mean, how much wider their faith can sweep when the evolutionary process is understood: telling them 'Your God is too small'.

*

There have been two main types of 'theodicy' during this century, in the English-speaking world. (1) There has been the 'Scale of Nature' type—tracing a line from Nature to Man to God. Relying on philosophers like Bergson, Lloyd Morgan, Smuts, Alexander and Whitehead, theologians such as Gore, William Temple, Tennant, and (the most distinguished of them) Father Thornton have used this method. Between types (1) and (2) have come, e.g. Karl Heim (with his 'analogy of dimensions' from physics to man: but then a sudden leap into existentialist psychology) and Paul Tillich. But (2) other philosophical theologians, more doubtful of the relevance of the sub-human, have concentrated upon the intellectual and moral factors in man as pointing to God. Such are A. E. Taylor, de Burgh, Marcel, and those influenced by 'existentialism' such as Farmer; but such is also Dr. A. M. Farrer. Dr. Farrer's criticism of type (1) is the most serious, and would seem to apply to Père Teilhard. He urged, in *Finite and Infinite* (1943) (and again at the end of *The Freedom of the Will* (1959)), that we are bound to be sceptical 'of the possibility of having sufficient insight into the mode of activity exercised by the other creatures' (i.e. below man) to be able to construct a 'scale of nature'; that, for instance, Alexander's 'elementary entities are personified abstractions . . . analogies derived negatively from our own being', upon which it is unsafe to build.[1]

Teilhard clearly falls within this category (1) but with a difference. For he is speaking not as a metaphysician but as a scientist in direct contact with the evidence: and the evidence points to a 'scale of nature'. But 'scale' is the wrong word: he is not at the top of a ladder looking back to the lower rungs which disappear in the mist. He is an observer, an observer *engagé*, watching a process unfold. His own expertise lay in the geology of mammals: but that required a deal of biology and not a little physics; indeed, chemistry too, and astrophysics. That is how he is able to work up from the 'barysphere' through the 'biosphere' to

[1] *Finite and Infinite*, pp. 44, 246.

the 'no-osphere'. And this is not the 'pathetic fallacy'—the reading back into sub-man of notions taken from man. For the evidence that points to evolution at all is the same evidence that points to a continuity of principle all the way up: the principle of 'complexity-consciousness'. Therefore Teilhard would not have agreed with Dr. Farrer that philosophical theology should confine itself to a study of the human will: he would have replied that our very understanding of the human will and its developments is incomplete except in the context of the total evolutionary process. And in discussing the future evolution of man he shows how the development of human personality is the continuation of the 'complexity-consciousness' principle at the human end of the evolutionary process: and therefore that the growth of a genuine community of persons, reconciling collectivity with respect for the individual, must be the next stage. And this means a growth in *love*—which marks the point where the Christian revelation, illuminating in a general way the whole process, becomes specifically and urgently relevant.

Teilhard's concerns put him at a point where he draws the fire from all sides—as M. Corte shows well. Scientists will question his extrapolations and his poetical language. Philosophers, especially our linguistic analysts, will wonder whether his metaphorical talk expresses true relations, or whether it doesn't rather smuggle mentalistic rabbits into physicalistic hats. Theologians will protest that the continuity he claims to see from the lowest point of evolution up to man and from there to 'Omega' (God?) is bound to lead to a heretical theology: for where is the Fall, and where is Grace, in this picture? And does it not put God Himself within the evolutionary process?

Teilhard is aware of all these criticisms, and tries to meet them. I do not think, myself, that his answers are wholly satisfactory: especially it seems that he was not fully aware of the *disruption* of sin and the '*skandalon*' of Grace. But even if true, I think it is important that Christians should see his failure here as part of his vocation. Again and again he complains how completely the non-scientist fails to enter into the world of the scientist: and he shows us the evidence as it appears to the eye of the trained naturalist. The time-scale and space-scale of the palaeontologist, as of the astronomer, is such that it must require an effort of the imagination, a conscious and unnatural switch of the attention, for him to take serious account of the sort of problems and evidence which appear crucial to the moralist or theologian. If we, in cold blood and at a distance, like to talk of the 'limitations of the scientific point of view', then we must go on to say that Père Teilhard's vocation was, by entering that world and working in it, precisely to share its 'limitations'. And there are limitations peculiar to the non-scientist too. Teilhard quotes, as an example, the remark of a Redemptorist Father in 1952, *à propos* the 'flying saucers' and their hypothetical passengers: 'If these rational beings' (the passengers) 'have escaped Original Sin, that is, if they possess corporal immortality such as Adam and Eve once enjoyed, it would be silly for our pilots to try and kill them. They would be unkillable.'[1] It was time that a Christian prophet came to say that the second limitation is more serious, more distorting, than the first.

And can we doubt that a vocation to a Christian priest to work and witness in this world of natural science is a vocation of great honour and importance? For it is a vocation above all to look, listen, and see (all of them Christian duties). One of the (to me) most vivid and revealing pictures of Père Teilhard is given by the geologist Helmut de Terra, who accompanied him on an expedition to India:

> 'I remember how, once when we had to make our way through thick vegetation almost like a jungle, Père Teilhard suddenly stopped dead as if he could hear something (the forest was silent). "The forest", he said, "is like the ocean, so full of hidden lives." He stayed there, quite motionless, enjoying the silence, and seemed to breathe in something of that hidden life which he loved so much.'[2]

MARTIN JARRETT-KERR, C.R.

## NOTE

Nicolas Corte (Leon Christiani) was born in France 1879, and obtained his doctorate in philosophy in Rome, 1930; Professor of modern and contemporary history at the Catholic University of Lyon, 1919–47, and Dean 1926–47. Author of seven or eight theological-historical books, the most recent being *Prèsence de Satan dans le monde moderne* ('The presence of Satan in the modern world').

The admirable English translation of Père Teilhard de Chardin's first volume, *The Phenomenon of Man* (Collins, 1959) appeared too late to be used in this book: but I have collated it with my version of quotations from Teilhard and adopted the same technical terms, for convenience.

[1] Letter, cit. Cuénot, p. 442.

[2] Cuénot, p. 234.

The substance of this Introduction appeared as a review-article in *Prism* (January 1960): I am indebted to the Editor for permission to use it here.

I am also profoundly indebted to Mr. R. M. Appleby, of the Department of Geology, University College, Cardiff, for his immense pains in reading my translation and correcting my scientific errors.

*Postscript*

English critics who judge Père Teilhard de Chardin purely on his first volume to appear in English (*The Phenomenon of Man*) would do well to reserve judgement on certain issues until more of his work has appeared over here. For example, more than one reviewer of *The Phenomenon of Man* has suggested that proof for the existence of life or man on other planets would destroy the main lines of P. Teilhard's evolutionary argument. It is worth pointing out that (as indeed M. Corte mentions briefly below, p. 62) Teilhard did, in fact, face that possibility. (See *Le Groupe Zoologique humain*, notes to p. 154 and 156.) What would destroy his argument would be the discovery on other planets of life that had not resulted from an evolutionary process. But it does not seem likely that evidence for that will be found.

Again, one reviewer (*Theology*, Feb. 1960) accuses P. Teilhard of 'flirting with Lamarck'. If by this is meant, flirting with the theory of the 'inheritance of acquired characteristics', then the accusation is not true. Indeed, in vol. III of Teilhard's works (*La Vision du Passé*) there is a chapter which contains a severe criticism of Professor F. Wood-Jones for his attempt to defend this very theory. But to use Lamarck as a hammer these days seems to be as disconcerting as playing croquet with flamingos; fortunately Teilhard is most careful not to get dragged into the game.

Finally, on several issues P. Teilhard came to see that his exposition in *The Phenomenon of Man* had been a trifle over-simplified; and his later essays, as well as the book (*Le Groupe Zoologique humain*) mentioned above, are to some extent correctives, or refinements, on his more popular argument there.

# INTRODUCTORY NOTE BY THE AUTHOR

A SHORT book must necessarily move within relatively narrow limits. Père Teilhard de Chardin died suddenly on April 10th, 1955, in New York, the evening of Easter day. We lack, and shall lack for some time, sufficient numbers of reactions to his work to be able to judge it finally, in spite of its great importance. It was Goethe who said that genuine greatness is that which time does not diminish but which, on the contrary, grows the further it spreads. We cannot predict with certainty what the judgement of time will be upon Teilhard's genius. Will he be, as some foresee, ranged in the company of his immortal compatriot, Pascal? Or will he be simply a great precursor, which is what he himself wanted? Only our grandchildren will be able to tell.

But it is not only the reactions to his work which we lack: it is also the documents. True, there are plenty of them. Perhaps there are even too many. Teilhard wrote a great deal. But what we lack is the publication of all his productions,[1] a complete and critical edition of all his works, arranged in exact chronological order, so that we could grasp the movement of his thought, note its increasing range, consider its progressive maturity, and determine its variations, even its contradictions through the course of the years.

Later on there will be three kinds of sources from which to write his life; his private correspondence, his writings, and the testimonies of those who knew him closely. What do we possess now of these three sources? His correspondence would be a most valuable source, at least for knowing the man, for entering into the heart of his life, his inner preoccupations, the intentions which guided him, the hopes he nourished. Of his correspondence we have, thanks to one of his near relatives, Mme Claude Aragonnès, a valuable collection. We shall try to make the best use of it in the following pages. But it is clear that this collection is far from being complete, that there must be extant many other letters which do not figure in it and which would probably be of

[1] A full list of these may be found in Cuénot, op. cit. (Tr.)

the greatest interest; and even among the letters in the Aragonnès collection a fair number are given only in précis-form, or in substantial digests which I am sure are perfectly accurate but which from a critical point of view cannot replace the actual texts.

As for the works, we already have a considerable dossier of them, but there remain others unpublished, and the chronology of the whole has still to be precisely established as also the circumstances in which each fragment was conceived, worked out, printed, or on the other hand kept back, for reasons which we should like to know.

Finally on Teilhard and his works we have appreciations, criticisms, essays, of which some are very penetrating. The works of Louis Cognet, of François-Albert Viallet, of Claude Tresmontant, the judgements of the abbé Breuil, of Mgr. Bruno de Solages, of M. Bergougnioux, of Claude Cuénot, and others already constitute an impressive ensemble, though we need to disentangle the sometimes contradictory elements in them. Nor can we neglect the critiques of such authorities as Père Bosio, Père Villain, articles in various periodicals, notably in *Ecclesia* (May 1956), in *La Table Ronde* (from June 1955), in *Revue nouvelle* (same date), in the *Revue de Paris* (February 1956), in the *Bulletin de Littérature ecclésiastique* (January-March 1956), etc.; though they may be of unequal value.

We shall try in this book to take account of everything valuable that has been said from various points of view on this large topic. It will be only a first draft, a glimpse, a very swift and summary account. But we hope it may serve at least to satisfy the legitimate curiosity of the general reader, and above all pave the way for more complete and so more authoritative studies which will better respond to the demands of the vast problems which are going to present themselves.

## METHOD

To make use of the documents which we already have available it seems both natural and inevitable to employ a chronological method, that is, one which follows the unfolding of the years step by step. We shall have to say how deeply Père Teilhard was concerned everywhere to follow the work of the moment, to consider time itself as an essential factor in the changing nature of all things, to see the whole universe advancing through what he calls, and what science now regularly calls, 'space-time'. The fundamental law of everything which experience enables us to reach is, according to him, the law of evolution. We shall have to make clear exactly what he means by that, and to say what we ought to think about his conviction in this matter. But in any case, even if the law of evolution were not—as he thought and as we think too—in large measure the law of all things, it remains certain that it is the law of the individuals we are, and that our ideas, our theories, our calculations, our judgements *evolve* with the experience that the years bring us. In an exposition of Teilhard's teachings, for instance, we cannot put passages from 1916 on the same level with passages from 1954. We shall see that he himself found the need, as he aged, to order, harmonize, and unify his ideas, even the most essential and constant ones. Here then chronology is bound up with the events themselves. It not only provides a tidy and reliable framework, it was a sort of active power, it helped to mature Père Teilhard's thought, and it played a leading part in the formation of his concepts. It constantly evolved, though always in the same direction. It is this evolution that we must, if not describe in minute detail—that would be too ambitious for a modest work like this—at least sketch out; and we must try to indicate for the sake of future syntheses whether—as we think—such syntheses could later be produced on the subject of his work.

Let us then set to at once, and go back to the beginnings of the wonderful career of this scientist and Christian thinker.

## CHAPTER ONE

# Childhood and Adolescence

NONE among the French Provinces is situated so completely in the heart of the country as the ancient Auvergne, the country of Vercingetorix and of Pascal. All the qualities of the race seem as it were to be condensed there, as if the fire of the local volcanoes had burnt them into the landscape. Foremost among these qualities we may point to the love of work, proverbial tenacity, originality, and the passion for adventure and conquest in every realm. All this is what we shall find in this man, the priest, the religious, whose progress we are going to follow.

He had a passion for research, which is the highest form of adventure and of conquest. He had a love for truth welded into a love of God.

### THE FAMILY CIRCLE

Pierre Teilhard de Chardin was the fourth of a family of eleven children. He was born in the château of Sarcenat, a little way to the west of Clermont-en-Auvergne. Sarcenat is not a commune: it is a small village, part of the communal district of Orcines, in which lies the mountain of Puy-de-Dôme. Pierre Teilhard's childhood was spent in one of the most beautiful mountainous sections of France. Not far from the château, to the west, beyond the plain of Fontaine-du-Berger, the picturesque summits of the peaks of Mongoulède rise in relief, rounded and verdant; Pariou with its fine crater; Nid-de-la-Poule, half blotted out by the enormous mass of Puy-de-Dôme which dominates the whole range. On the east you can see the lovely city of Clermont, clustered round its glorious cathedral; and more to the north the grassy plain of Limagne, one of the most fertile in France. The village of Orcines has a fourteenth-century church, frequented by generations of the Teilhard de Chardin family.

The child whose life we are unfolding underwent, like many other children, at first without knowing it, the subtle influences of his family circle, of his father, his mother, his brothers and sisters, of the château itself, the relaxed atmosphere that reigned there, the courteous manners which everybody adopted, the Christian faith that was professed, the serious attitude to work, the intelligent curiosity, the taste for wide horizons: all these were soaked in and handed down like a sacred inheritance from age to age.

It is from Père Teilhard himself that we learn what he considered his particular debt to his father and mother.

His father, Emmanuel Teilhard de Chardin, was a man of powerful mind who took a great deal of trouble over his children, watched over them from their first spiritual awakening, and managed their education until their going to school. When he died, 11 February 1932, his son Pierre happened to be in China taking part in what has been called 'The Yellow Expedition'.[1] This death, which affected him considerably, was the occasion for his admitting that he owed many things to his father; and he mentioned in particular 'certain precise aspirations, no doubt, but still more a sort of fundamental equilibrium on which all the rest was built'. By that he evidently meant a very French desire for clarity, for logic, for harmony in ideas, and especially for agreement between the religious ideal and the acquisitions of human knowledge. The agreement, this 'equilibrium', were the objects of his impassioned research throughout his life. And when he speaks of 'certain precise aspirations' we are convinced that by this he meant his particular scientific vocation. As he spent the greater part of the year in the country, in his massive, squat château of Sarcenat, Emmanuel Teilhard had given his son a taste for natural history collections. It is not difficult to see in this the first awakening to a unique scientific vocation in the son, Pierre.

He was still in China, in Pekin, when he learned of the death of his mother on February 7th, 1936. And he wrote about her, 'My dear and saintly mother, to whom I owe the deepest parts of me.' This means that from very young days great powers of affection developed in his soul which he never lost and that this affection was chiefly kindled into existence by his mother.

In writing the life of this distinguished scholar we must never forget that the love of God predominated, as he believed, over all others, and

[1] *La Croisière jaune* (see below) was an archaeological-geographical-geological expedition through central Asia from Persia to China, to which Pierre Teilhard was attached as the accredited geologist.

that all his own life had its 'axis'—as he liked to say—in God, whether as God in Himself or as the sovereign author of nature.

## FIRST IMPRESSIONS

Most of us have only very occasional flashes of memory from our childhood's years. For all of us the possibility of memory is bound up with the possibilities of forgetfulness. We have to discard an infinite number of impressions of our youth in order to preserve just a few. And we are often surprised at the ones that do survive. Indeed psychiatrists, rightly or wrongly, attach great importance to this selection which our memory makes in the most distant past of our lives. It is possible too that this selection of memories may be influenced by our later tastes and choices.

What were Père Teilhard's memories, then, later on and towards the end of his life? Claude Cuénot, in *La Table Ronde* (June 1955), reports: 'From the age of four or five—so he told us in a conversation (12 July 1950)—he already had a "general cosmic sense (the consistency of the whole)". And later "the cosmic came to be concentrated in the human, in the Christly".' This first indication is given more precision in a manuscript of thirty very closely written pages, which Teilhard called *The Heart of the Matter*. This text dates from 1950. So it was written at the age when one who has become an old man likes to go back to his most distant 'source'.

## THE TWO APPEALS

What he sees most clearly in his own past is a double appeal, from Matter and from God. But we must let him speak for himself here and quote at some length:

'However far I go back in my childhood, the most characteristic and the most familiar thing I find in my inner attitude is the yearning or irresistible need for some "One Thing Sufficient and Necessary".' [The capitals are Teilhard's own.] 'To be completely at ease, to be entirely happy I needed to know that "Some One Essential Thing" existed, to which everything else was only accessory or even an ornament. I needed to know it, and to be able to play endlessly with the consciousness of this existence. Indeed, if as I look back I am able to recognize myself at all and to follow my path, it is only by the trace of this note, this tinge, or this particular savour in my life. And this is something which, however little of it one has once experienced, it is impossible to mistake for any other of the passions of the soul—neither the joy of knowledge nor that of discovery nor that of creating nor of loving; not so much because it is different from all of them, but because it is of a higher order and contains all of them.'

One can't help recalling, on reading these lines, St. Teresa of Avila, while still quite young, saying over and over again for hours in a sort of ecstasy, with her brother Rodrigue, *Para siempre! siempre! siempre!*—'For ever! Ever! Ever!' What she too wanted, and what she went to look for in the convent, was the One Thing Sufficient, the One Thing Necessary, that something essential without which life is not worth living. The whole of Christianity is a response to this primary need of human nature.

But how did this need in his being find its expression, in the case of young Pierre Teilhard? This is where the two 'appeals' burst in on him so strangely.

He goes on: 'I was certainly no more than six or seven when I began to feel myself drawn by Matter—or more exactly by something that "shone" at the heart of Matter. At this age when I suppose other children feel their first "sentiment" for a person or for art or for religion, I was affectionate, well-behaved, even pious. That is, catching it from my mother, I loved "the little lord Jesus" dearly. But in reality my genuine self was quite elsewhere. To find out about this you would have had to watch me as I withdrew, always secretly and without a word, without even thinking that there was anything worth saying about it to anyone, to contemplate, indeed, to possess, to savour the existence of my "God, Iron". Yes, just that: Iron. I can still see with extraordinary clarity the whole series of my "idols". In the country a plough-key which I hid away carefully in a corner of the yard. In the town, the hexagonal head of a metal staple which stuck out at the level of the nursery floor and which I took possession of. Later on, little shell-splinters which I collected lovingly on a nearby shooting range.'

We can recognize here the shooting range of la Fontaine-du-Berger, which is in fact quite close to the château of Sarcenat, in the direction of Puy-de-Dôme.

The reader may find this all very childish. Certainly: but Père Teilhard, then aged sixty-nine and a learned man known all over the world, did not hesitate to write: 'I can't help smiling today when I think of these pranks. Yet at the same time I am forced to recognize that in this instinctive movement which made me truly speaking *worship* a little piece of metal, there was a strong sense of self-giving and a whole train of obligations all mixed up together; and my whole spiritual life has merely been the development of this.'

So it was he himself who performed the psychological analysis of his very early spiritual condition.

## FROM SCHOOL TO NOVITIATE

When young Pierre reached the age for secondary education he was sent by his parents to the college of Mongré, run by the Jesuit Fathers, near Villefranche-sur-Saône. This college had the best reputation from the point of view of discipline, of serious studies and of social milieu. The house is very well situated at the bottom of Promenade Hill: from there there is a view, on one side, of the foothills of the monts d'Or and of Beaujolais, and on the opposite side, of the Jura, and even on some days of the peaks of the Alps. It was a religious and aristocratic establishment and very select. The years Pierre Teilhard spent at Mongré must be regarded as decisive for the direction of his life. It was there that he chose his future. It was there he opted for the austere and sacrificial life of a religious. He had in fact to go from the Jesuit college at Mongré to the Jesuit novitiate at Aix-en-Provence. How did this development happen during these hours which decided his destiny? We do not know, and that will be one of the points for his future biographers to clear up. All we have been told so far is that at Mongré Pierre Teilhard was known as a quiet, pious and rather dreamy pupil. This last characteristic probably hides a number of things. We are not surprised to learn that this man of science, this person—so highly practical both by taste and in performance—was also a 'dreamer'; no doubt that means that he was often lost in his thoughts, that he pondered over the profoundest problems away from everybody else, that he asked the most serious questions, weighed, calculated deliberately day after day in his spiritual life, his prayer and his work too, what he ought to do with this great and unique possession of his, his life—weighed it all in the sight of God, and with the help of his confessor. At the age when most pupils, even good ones, are preoccupied chiefly with how to pull off their baccalauréat and so open up a career for themselves in the world, Pierre Teilhard without neglecting his studies and in fact successfully passing the relevant examinations, already had a keen desire to serve God, to put his young energies at the service of his faith. That is what led him, as we have said, to the college of the novitiate, which he entered in 1899 at the age of eighteen. He must have taken his exams in his stride, for we hear nothing about them. But we can guess two things: first, that he must have branched off, as they used to do then, in philosophy towards the sciences and not towards pure letters; and second, that he was entered for the science degree, probably at Aix or Marseille, which allowed him to do only one year of military service instead of three—which was the rule then until the law of 1905 put everyone under a uniform term of two years.

We do not know where he spent his year's service. Wherever it was, it was no doubt in the Medical Corps, for in 1914 during the general mobilization we find him a corporal stretcher-bearer in a regiment of Moroccan Zouaves.

## TO AIX AND JERSEY

At Aix-en-Provence the most influential person was a philosopher of the front rank, Maurice Blondel. His thesis, *L'Action*, which dated from 1893, had created a sensation. It was almost inevitable that young Teilhard should want to and be able to make contact with the celebrated Catholic thinker. In fact it is certain, as Claude Cuénot tells us, that he exchanged ideas with him and even corresponded with him. And Claude Cuénot adds, 'Teilhard's philosophy of action can be put into the same category (namely that of Blondel) through its attempt to define the transcendent affirmations which alone make action possible.' We are of the same opinion as Claude Cuénot that there are striking parallels between Blondel's theses and those we find in Teilhard. But in detail the differences between the two systems of thought are immense. Blondel sets off from a profound psychological analysis and never leaves the realm of man himself. Teilhard only reaches man through the whole universe, and it is from the whole of the universe that he deduces the immanent need for God.

In any case, we should be betraying our own chosen method if we attributed to Teilhard's stay of only a few years from 1899, even a rough sketch of the later 'vision' of the world which he gradually formed in his mind.

Following the law on Associations of July 1st, 1901, the Jesuits were afraid that they would never receive authorization from a hostile government; so they wisely moved their novitiate from Aix-en-Provence to the island of Jersey. Teilhard was among the juniors who followed their masters into exile. And it was in Jersey that there occurred a crisis which was both exceptional and vital for him.

## THE CRISIS IN JERSEY

We must note carefully what Teilhard himself has to say about this 'crisis'. We know that from childhood two appeals had come to him, two loves had competed for the mastery. No doubt young Pierre had given up his juvenile 'idols' long ago, those bits of iron or shell-splinters collected at la Fontaine-du-Berger. But his two loves, for nature and for God, were still there in the deepest part of him. And for him nature meant scientific research—which he later on declared to be a third dimension, a third infinity in our Universe, along with the infinitely tiny and the inter-galactic infinitely great. But must the two loves be in opposition? Must one choose between them? Ought Abraham to sacrifice his son to prove his faith and love to God? The crisis can be summed up in the dilemma: Matter or Spirit? Can the two terms be reconciled with each other? It was a poignant and an urgent question for the young Jesuit. He tells us about it in his manuscript of 1950, *The Heart of the Matter*. At this date he had coined a new vocabulary which we shall have to explore. He had become used to creating new expressions, inventing neologisms which put off quite a number of his readers and which he did not know of in his youth. But this is how he interpreted his drama at twenty-five years old:

'There was a struggle going on at the very centre of my being between the God "on high" and a sort of new God "in front", due to the fact that the cosmic Sense and the Christly Sense definitely coexisted in my heart and irresistibly drew towards each other.

'I can find the first traces of this opposition during my college days, in my pathetic attempt to reconcile the evangelical fervour (which was certainly too narrow) of the *Imitation*, which was the nourishment of my morning prayers, with my attraction towards Nature. Later, when a junior at Jersey, I seriously pondered the eventuality of a complete renunciation of the study of stones . . . in order to dedicate myself entirely to so-called "supernatural" activities. I was saved from "going off the rails" at this moment by the robust good sense of Father T.' (His Master of Novices.) 'In fact Father T. in this case limited himself to assuring me that the God of the Cross expected the "natural" expansion of my being just as much as its sanctification, without explaining to me how or why.'

This directive from the Master of Novices, which was entirely in the logic of Catholic Christianity and in line with the Ignatian tradition, was enough to calm the interior storms of the young religious. But it is to his great and lasting credit that, whatever the difficulties, he never allowed these two loves to grow as if separated from each other by a watertight compartment. He would not rest until he had brought them into agreement with each other. In fact, that was to be the ideal and the task of his whole life.

In the text already quoted he says of this crisis which he had just surmounted: 'It was enough to leave me the two ends of the line in my hands. And that's how I got things straight.'

In another text, called *Modern Unbelief*, he made clear what from now on he would see as his highest goal to pursue, in his vocation as a Jesuit: 'The world is in process of being converted of its own accord to a sort of natural Religion of the Universe, which turns it severely away from the God of the Gospels: this is what its "unbelief" consists in. Let us convert this conversion itself, turn it one degree further, by showing, through the whole of our life, that only the Christ *in quo omnia constant* (in whom all things consist) can animate and direct the newly-glimpsed progress of the Universe. Then by prolonging the line of what makes for today's unbelief, we may come perhaps to tomorrow's faith.'

These are fine words. He had managed, thanks to his wise and perceptive Master of Novices, to achieve the unification in himself. Now he could follow both his irresistible attractions at once. Abraham will not have to sacrifice his child. For Pierre Teilhard de Chardin the service of God will find its way through scientific research pushed to its extreme limit. We must not forget this, for everything in his life can be explained by this and this alone. One day he was able to write, in the same context, 'In fact, and even at the highest point of my spiritual trajectory, I only find myself completely at ease when bathed in an ocean of Matter.'

Research: this is the aspect under which he thinks of Science. It is something quite different from pleasure in knowledge: it is the passion for discovery, for penetrating the mystery of things and thereby also the mystery of God. As we were saying a moment ago, for him it is a third infinity which lies before man.

We have followed him up to 1905. He is twenty-six now. He is fully developed. He is at peace with himself. The God 'in front' (i.e. of scientific research) will from now on be equally for him the God 'on high' (i.e. of faith, of adoration and love). In the next chapter we shall see his first scientific essays, which are also his first writings, the first manifestations of his precocious genius as a thinker.

## CHAPTER TWO

# First Labours and First Writings

### LECTURER IN CAIRO

BY entering the Society of Jesus, Pierre Teilhard had enrolled himself in an Institution that could be called world-wide. It had been so from its very first beginnings. Ignatius Loyola had envisaged a Missionary Institution at the very time that Catholic missions for the first time embraced the whole globe. Jesuits had made their way as far as Japan and China on one side, and to Brazil and Mexico, and finally all South America on the other. Pierre Teilhard besides his passion for nature had a passion for travel, which indeed is only an aspect of the former; by force of circumstances he was going to be able to satisfy his appetite for the wide world. More than one Jesuit in his time might be famed as a great traveller throughout the world—Père Albert Valensin, for instance, to mention only one; but we think that Père Teilhard must have beaten all the records in this sphere. The number of countries he visited and the number of miles covered during fifty years of life in Religion is astonishing.

In 1905 he had finished his studies in philosophy and theology, and his time of spiritual formation. He was appointed teacher of physics at Cairo by his superiors. Note that he had not yet started to specialize. The 'stuff of things' appeared to him when he was a child under the shining form of metal. But he loved *stone* in general. His first steps were in the direction of geology and geography. There, he said, he found 'the primacy of Matter—Matter expressing itself in Mineral and Rock'. It was only little by little that he came to Palaeontology and then to Prehistory. It was in Jersey that he had his first experience of field-work. His travel in Egypt excited him very much, both at the sight of nature in quite a new guise, swallowed up in light and heat, and at the novel aspects of geological stratification. In addition to that he had by the nature of his job fundamentally to revise his physics, since he had to teach it. St. Francis de Sales has well said that the best way of learning is to teach. And this was at the very time when sensational discoveries were being made in the realms of physics. Radium was being discussed, and its properties which till then had been unknown in the world of matter. The unexplored domain of the atom had been reached, and already there was talk about the eventual possibility of what today is called 'atomic fission'.

Of course the young professor was only at the threshold of 'nuclear' studies. At Cairo he taught what later on he was to call 'a very elementary kind of physics'—which he was the first to laugh over.

There was one danger at this time, which he escaped only by the breadth of his inner ambition: what he called 'the collector's midden'. Nearly all beginners in science go through it. They collect facts, observations, objects, pebbles, plants, fossils, much as others collect stamps or butterflies. But Teilhard wanted something quite different. Details never cluttered up and concealed the whole. He was never one to fail to see the wood for the trees.

In his autobiography, *The Heart of the Matter* (1950), from which we have already quoted, he describes the path of his scientific curiosity. We have seen how he started off from geology; 'But', he says, 'all round it was, almost incidentally, the growing appeal of vegetable and animal Nature; and deeper down, one fine day, came my initiation into the less tangible, but no less tempting, grandeurs revealed by the researches of physics. *On each side of Matter stood Life and Energy: the three pillars of my inward vision and happiness.*' The italics are ours at the end: but the quotation marks, as always, are his.

## EVOLUTION

It was about this time, too, that the idea of evolution developed in him, 'just at the right moment', he says, 'like a seed sprung from I don't know where'. He had in fact read Bergson's *Creative Evolution*, which came out in 1906. He tells us about it, in these lines taken from the same text: 'I remember clearly having read *Creative Evolution* with avidity at this time. But although I didn't very well understand at this period what exactly Bergson's *Durée* meant—and in any case it was not sufficiently convergent to satisfy me—I can see clearly that the effect of these passionate pages on me was merely, at the right moment and in a flash, to stir up a fire that was already burning in my heart and mind.'

It was not then from Bergson that he borrowed his idea of Evolution. Nor was it from Darwin or Lamarck. We shall see, in fact, that his idea of Evolution cannot be confused with the 'transformism'[1] of species, but is something much wider, much more primitive and wholesale, more like the very law of the Universe created in Space-Time. But once he had formed this idea, it never ceased to grow and to branch out.

## AT HASTINGS

After this he was recalled from Cairo. He was not yet a priest, and so he still had to complete his tests preparatory to the priesthood. The Jesuit Scholasticate was established at Hastings, in Sussex. And there, while deep in his final studies of advanced theology between 1909 and 1912, he completed the process which he describes thus: 'During my years of theology at Hastings, that is just after experiencing the marvels of Egypt, little by little I grew more and more conscious, less as an abstract notion than as a *presence*, of a profound, ontological total drift of the Universe around me: so conscious of this that it filled my whole horizon.'

We must understand right away that for him Evolution, something much more than a transformation of species, is precisely this general 'drift' of all things, under the pressure of the Creator. And taken in this sense, Evolution was not for him a laboratory acquisition or a scientific hypothesis, but a vital reality, felt in his innermost being, and as he says again, a magic key 'which kept coming back to my mind, like a refrain, or a taste, a promise and an appeal'.

Indeed seldom has a philosophy—or as he liked to say, a *Weltanschauung*, a total vision of things—been a more personal, more intimate and more living thing than this idea was for Teilhard de Chardin.

## HIS FIRST ARTICLE

It was also during this period, after his return from Egypt, that his first article was accepted and published in *Etudes*.[2] The name of the journal alone is a guarantee of something serious and solid. It is also a good proof of the high opinion that the Fathers in Paris had of their young colleague, who was still in his twenty-eighth year.

[1] Throughout his work Père Teilhard uses 'transformism' as equivalent to 'evolution'—not implying Lamarckianism.

[2] January 1909, vol. 118.

This article, twenty-two full pages, is interesting on more than one count. First, for the subject-matter, then for its tone, its style, the spirit in which it is written. The subject is: 'The Miracles of Lourdes and Canonical Investigations.' Père Teilhard recalls that in 1905 Pope Pius X had expressed the wish that regular canonical procedures should be instituted to establish the reality of the miracles at Lourdes. The Pope's wish was followed. Père Teilhard outlines twenty-five canonical procedures already carried through to their conclusion by thirteen bishops, twelve of them French and one Belgian. He shows that the preliminary enquiries were conducted by qualified doctors. Their rôle was not to say whether there had been a miracle or not, but only to declare that in their opinion the facts indicated as miraculous could not be explained by natural laws. It was only for the ecclesiastical authorities then to draw the conclusion namely that these facts could only be miracles, that is, effects of a merciful intervention by God, by-passing the laws of nature. Père Teilhard enters fully into the thought of the bishops. He approves of the processes and of their conclusions without hesitation or reserve and obviously with satisfaction. And yet his intention is to look at the thing entirely from the scientific point of view. From the first few sentences of his article it is clear that it is a scientist who is speaking. He contrasts, with mild surprise, the alacrity with which experts observe, classify, catalogue facts when these fit into their established categories, with their off-handedness, their hesitation and their obvious irritation when they are face to face with facts which refer to prayer or to faith, in fact, to the 'supernatural'. The opposite ought to be the case. Integrity, loyalty and sincerity are involved. Père Teilhard asks why they refuse to come to any conclusions in such cases: 'Yet they could do so quite logically. The things concerned are observable, they can be precisely studied, just like an eclipse of the sun. But official science is silent on the matter; it feigns ignorance, or retreats before the explanation, dodging phenomena which it finds embarrassing; and so it is disloyal to its reputation for impartiality and for absolute respect for facts.'

The whole article is written in this vein. Teilhard's style is quite different from that which we shall meet in his last works. Later it will be crammed with neologisms, as if ordinary words were inadequate to express thoughts which overflow normal barriers, which are stretched to their utmost. In Père Teilhard's earlier articles, on the other hand, his expression is simple, easy, fluent, classic in its purity. It avoids any too blatantly technical terms and remains always within the grasp of ordinary readers.

We shall not dwell on this first publication of Père Teilhard's, but we should like to preserve the following passage, which reveals one of the main hinges of his later teaching. In refuting the objection, according to which the 'miracles' of Lourdes are only due to a flow of nervous energy which exists, more or less, in everybody, he writes:

'Here is a fundamental error of reasoning, and also a mistake as to fact. Modern science has established that there is a continuity in the field of biology, as in physics and in history; it claims to have demonstrated that the properties of beings do not appear suddenly, are not enclosed within a category, but extend to a notable degree beyond the classes which possess them, and go shading off into a penumbra which is unreachable at its limits. *We shall not attempt to prove that there is discontinuity between life and matter, intelligence and life. But maintaining the scientific attitude in general, we must point out that the appearance of certain effects implies that, by the principle of causality, they have reached a critical point*: a lever may remain motionless under the pressure of one kilogram, but will be lowered by a higher degree of pressure.'

We have put the essential lines of this quotation in italics. Later we shall come to speak of this *critical threshold*, of which the young author speaks here. Later he will make it one of the bases for his explanation of the world.

## TOWARDS PALAEONTOLOGY

It may be during this year, 1909, that Père Teilhard, who up till now had limited his work to geology, though without strictly specializing in it, acquired a taste for palaeontology, which would later lead him on to Prehistory. True, all his life he continued to love 'geologizing' as he called it, and he could usually be seen armed with the professional hammer. But now he made contact with a prehistorian of the front rank, Marcellin Boule, a man of Auvergne like him, though from Cantal; he was the director of the Palaeontological Laboratory of the Paris Museum. The abbé Henri Breuil, speaking on the radio on November 21st, 1955, gave the details thus:

'I have been asked to speak to you about the late Père Teilhard and his book, *Le Phénomène humain*—no doubt because I was one of his oldest friends. I met him at the Palaeontological Laboratory of the Museum, where Professor Boule introduced me. He was then, about 1909, I think, a young Jesuit novice, with a remarkably live and versatile intelligence, wonderfully approachable. From that time we always kept in touch, so far as our careers allowed it.'

The abbé Breuil, whose reputation as a prehistorian is unequalled, said again, in an article in *La Table Ronde*: 'It must have been about 1910 or a little before that Père Teilhard de Chardin was introduced to me, in the Palaeontological Laboratory in the Museum, by Professor Boule.' And he goes on that it was Père Teilhard who took him, with other young prehistorians, in the summer of 1913, to the excavations in the north of Spain directed by Dr. H. Obermaier and P. Wernert. 'That was certainly his first initiation into a full-scale prehistoric excavation.'

It appears that in the meanwhile Père Teilhard had finished his scholasticate at Hastings and been ordained priest in 1912. So it was not till after that date that he was able to devote himself more regularly to researches in prehistory. He was attached to the Museum of Natural History in Paris, under the direction of Boule, from 1912 to 1914. It was then that he found himself mixed up in what is today called the 'Piltdown fraud'.

'It was about the same time,' says the abbé Breuil, in *La Table Ronde*, 'that is in 1913, that during one period of his novitiate'—or rather, scholasticate—'he met the geologists and palaeontologists of London, Professor Smith-Woodward among them. And so he took part, at Piltdown, in Dawson's excavations, and found the famous canine, "in the sieve", as he wrote to me quite recently. He did not suspect, any more than the other victims of Dawson's extremely skilful fraud, that the stratum had been "cooked": and indeed the whole scientific body was taken in by it for half a century.'

We know that the fraud was not uncovered till 1953. But Père Teilhard could never believe that Dawson himself was not the first to be deceived by the 'cooking'.

The young prehistorian had had bad luck in his first discovery. He made up for it brilliantly later.

## THE 1914 WAR

Meanwhile the First World War broke out. France recalled all her citizens to their duty. Pierre Teilhard responded with enthusiasm to the sudden call. For this whole period we have valuable evidence from Max Bégouën, one of the sons of the prehistorian Count Bégouën, himself devoted from his childhood to this kind of study. He first met Père Teilhard in the summer of 1915.

'I was doing my military washing in the pond on the farm called Killem on which we were billeted, near the Belgian frontier, he wrote in *La Table Ronde*, June 1955, 'when a tall, thin corporal of the sharpshooters came up to me.

'"Max Bégouën?"

'"That's me."

'"I'm Teilhard," said the soldier.

'I started. "Are you the man of the Piltdown excavations, then?" He smiled, and told me that he had discovered through Marcellin Boule and the abbé Breuil that my brother and I were in the R.I.C.M., which along with the 4th Zouaves made up a brigade. Teilhard was a stretcher-bearer in the Zouaves and he had come at once to contact us.'

But what is most worth recording from Max Bégouën's account is the description he gives of Teilhard the stretcher-bearer under shell-fire:

'Père Teilhard's behaviour under fire', he says, 'is shown us both by the evidence of his comrades and officers, and by his fine mentions in despatches and his decorations—croix de guerre, military medal, Légion d'honneur. I can testify to his calm courage, his mastery over danger which communicated a sense of peace all round him. The North-African sharpshooters of his regiment thought he was protected by his *baraka*.[1] The curtains of machine-gun fire and the hail of bombardments both seemed to pass him by. During the attacks of 25 September at Artois, my brother was wounded, and as he wandered on the battle-field he saw a single stretcher-bearer rising up in front of him, and he, for it was Teilhard, accomplished his mission quite imperturbably under terrible fire. My brother has often told me that it seemed like a miracle to find the khaki silhouette of a priest coming running towards him, to bandage him and take him to the first-aid post.—"I thought I had seen the appearance of a messenger from God."

'I once asked Père Teilhard, "What do you do to keep this sense of calm during the battle? It looks almost as if you don't see the danger and that fear doesn't touch you?"

'He answered, with that serious but friendly smile which gave such a human warmth to his words, "If I'm killed I shall just change my state, that's all."

'The conviction and assurance, as well as the simplicity with which this statement of faith was made gave me quite a shock. We were still right in the middle of the war, and God alone knows how much carnage there was. So what he expressed was an attitude of mind quite deliberately adopted and lived out, his rule of life.'

[1] *Baraka*: a Moslem Arabic word for 'spiritual stature' or 'supernatural quality': e.g. 'Gandhi had immense *baraka*; Nehru has almost none'—John Gunther, *Inside Africa*, p. 60.

## A VITAL EXPERIENCE

But Max Bégouën's account does not end there. What he says next throws perhaps even more light on the rest of Père Teilhard's life.

Max Bégouën had found his childhood faith tottering during his first contacts with Science. Prehistory seemed suddenly to demolish all the data given in the Bible, and consequently the faith which is dependent on biblical revelation. 'A few years before the war', Max Bégouën recounts, 'Prehistory had shown me the longevity of Man on the earth, and the existence of fossilized human remains. Questions arose in my mind to which nobody had been able to give me a satisfactory answer.'

The young man consulted his director in vain. He was a well-educated and highly intelligent person, a man full of goodwill too; but he was a total stranger to scientific questions. His answers to the anxious questions of his penitent were 'so utterly conventional, banal and evasive', that the young man, who was only eighteen, was confirmed in his conviction that there could be no possible link between Science and the Faith, since there was an irreducible contradiction between them.

As a result of the shocking experiences of the war, of a severe wound received at the front, the near prospect of death, a long and demoralizing stay in hospital, the climate of exhaustion, fatigue, bitterness and revolt —these are his own words—in which the war came to a close, Max Bégouën ended up, spiritually speaking, right off the rails. And it was then, in the autumn of 1919, after demobilization, that the friendship he had made at the front with Père Teilhard bore fruit. He had dined with him at a relative's house, behind the Church of Saint-Augustin.

'We took leave of our hostess', he says, 'and at about nine o'clock we went off with the Father to catch the métro to the Madeleine. It was raining and cold. Walking beside him I told him that I had lost my faith for some time, and I explained the reasons. Very simply, with that kindness and affection which never seemed to leave him, *he expounded to me his ideas on Creation, the meaning of Evolution, the supreme and active part played in the Evolution of the Cosmos by Christ*. From nine o'clock till midnight, walking up and down in the rain between Saint-Augustin and the Madeleine, the Father gave me explanations which threw light on everything. He gave me the answer I had so long been waiting for.

'That evening', concludes Max Bégouën, 'I came to life, tottering like Lazarus coming out of the tomb at the Lord's command "Come forth!" It was a dazzling experience which soon changed my life from top to bottom. . . .'

I don't think it is rash to conjecture that the effect of such an experience was just as important for Père Teilhard as for his young friend. He was an anthropologist, a seeker not so much for fossils as for living souls, or souls to be made alive. And now he had been able to try out on a brilliant mind the penetrative power of the reflections which were already so much a part of his own life. The words we have printed in italics in the quotation given above are in fact a summary of everything we shall find in his writings, and above all in that work which embraces all his others, *The Phenomenon of Man* (*Le Phénomène humain*).

But of course a shattering experience like that had wider effects than the mere case of Max Bégouën. 'Now that he has left us', concluded Max Bégouën, 'we can guess at, though we can't measure, the extent of his influence. He was truly an apostle, and in particular an apostle of Christ "to the gentiles". His concern for the greater glory of God turned him into an explorer and soldier, the kind that goes in search of new countries to extend there the power of their monarch. . . . In my own varied travels I have often come across, quite by accident, strangers who, through the most improbable series of coincidences, have heard the voice of Père Teilhard, quite outside the "parish boundary", and have responded to it. . . .'

This is a witness which we ought to bear in mind when we have later to expound, and perhaps criticize, Père Teilhard's teachings. We shall think then of all the people he has won back for Christ, and we shall be very chary of disturbing them by careless accusations or unqualified condemnation.

From the Christian point of view, which we frankly adopt here, we can never be sufficiently grateful to those priests, like Jean Guibert the Sulpician with his book on *Origins* (1897), or the abbé Breuil, the two abbés Bouysonnie, the abbé Obermaier, and Teilhard de Chardin himself, who threw themselves into the study of Prehistory in order to take part in it as experts and to keep contact between Science and Faith. And in those early stages this was a commendable thing to do, as we shall see.

### A PUBLICATION OF PÈRE TEILHARD'S

In the foregoing pages we have omitted to speak of an important article by Père Teilhard called 'Prehistory and its Development', published in *Etudes* (5 January 1913).

Here he mainly described the recent works of Dr. Hugo Obermaier, a man of German origin, himself also a priest, and appointed ever since its foundation to the Institute of Human Palaeontology in Paris, by Prince Albert of Monaco.

His account is sober and precise, written in the same classical language as the article on the 'Miracles of Lourdes', and we only quote that part which contains a sort of declaration of faith in the science of Prehistory itself:

'There was a time', he writes, 'when Prehistory deserved to be regarded with suspicion or treated as a joke. With their often fanciful reconstructions, and the anti-Christian tendency of their theses, the first practitioners of Prehistory seemed to want deliberately to provoke the common opposition of experts and believers, and this opposition they certainly stirred up. They were treated tacitly as sectarians or fanatics. Today this attitude of coldness and disdain is no longer appropriate. Now that the facts that have been collected provide a wider basis for serious reconstructions; and now too that a less hysterical attitude towards the relationship between Science and Faith prevails, and we can show that religious truth is well protected against the constant twisting and turning which happens to the experimental science of man, it has become quite unpardonable to ignore or to denigrate the work of Prehistory. Prehistory is gradually becoming a true and exact science. . . .'

And Père Teilhard at once produced evidence of this publication of the first thirteen parts of Obermaier's great work 'Man of all Times' (*Der Mensch aller Zeiten*).

Teilhard's expressions seem to suggest that he saw Prehistory as a sort of battle-front. And he intended to bring to it the same quiet courage, the same imperturbable assurance which, we have seen, he took into the front and into the face of death, during the war.

### A FACULTY PROFESSORSHIP

The war itself did not completely interrupt Père Teilhard's scientific studies. Marcellin Boule had managed recently to acquire for the Museum he directed, a fine collection of fossil vertebrae, coming from the Phosphorites or phosphates of lime (mostly 'apatites') at Quercy; and he had put Père Teilhard on to study the group of carnivorous mammals. Teilhard had written a memorandum on this subject in which we can already find the idea which becomes more precise in his mind later on: the tendency of the world of living things to branch out as it goes on. In 1916, in the middle of the war, he started on a new essay, a study of the little primates of the Tertiary, based also on the Phosphorites of Quercy. Here a new idea, which was also going to develop in this thought later, appeared: namely that in this group the most marked trend had been in the direction leading to the largest brain.

In 1919, immediately after demobilization, Père Teilhard again took up his place in the Palaeontological Laboratory of the Museum, and under Boule's direction he prepared his thesis for Doctor of Science on the *Mammals of the Lower Eocene in France*. This was a study of the very first mammals, going back, after the monsters of the Secondary Era, to the beginning of the Tertiary, that is, between seventy and fifty thousand years before our time. An amateur palaeontologist had discovered some of these, a few years before, in the neighbourhood of Rheims. The war in the trenches enabled Père Teilhard partly to take up his researches again and to correct more than one false attribution. He showed remarkable astuteness in interpreting the remains of often very fragmentary fossils, and to relate his discoveries to those which had already been classified in the Tertiary fauna of Europe and North America. Now he could add to the mammals of France those of the Eocene period in Belgium. What was most striking in Père Teilhard's thesis was the enthusiasm and assurance with which he adopted the evolutionary theory. Marcellin Boule himself, who fundamentally agreed with him, found himself outstripped by the audacity of his pupil's thought. A lively controversy with Vialleton ensued, sometimes in oral discussions sometimes in articles. Père Teilhard's thesis, which he presented in 1922, was quite an event. The Institut Catholique of Paris offered him the same year a Professorship of Geology.

But Père Teilhard did not on that account abandon Palaeontology or Prehistory. In the interval, in 1921, *Etudes* (March) had published a short but substantial article by him on 'Fossil Men: *à propos* a recent Book'. Here he presented to the general public, with all the praise it deserved, Marcellin Boule's very important work which had just appeared, and which was to make a great impression by the clarity of its exposition and the extent of its documentation. We shall only quote the conclusions of this article. After having noted that, according to Boule, 'our race, by its history, is of a piece with, and continuous with, the world which bears it', he observed that certain of the author's expressions could not 'enter into Christian thought just as they stand'. And then he added a page of great significance:

'The letter of the Bible shows us the Creator fashioning the body of man out of earth. Conscientious observation of the world leads us to see today that by this "earth" *we must understand a substance that has been slowly elaborated by the totality of things*,' (italics ours), 'in such a way that man, we should say, has been drawn out not exactly from a little bit of amorphous matter, but by a long effort of the whole "Earth". In spite of the serious difficulties which still prevent us from reconciling them fully with certain more commonly accepted pictures of Creation, these views, which were familiar to St. Gregory of Nyssa and to St. Augustine, ought not to upset us. We cannot yet say exactly in what terms it will be, but without sacrificing a single fragment of the data, whether revealed or definitely demonstrated, little by little an agreement is appearing quite naturally between science and dogma, in this contentious field of human origins. As we wait for it, we must avoid rejecting the smallest ray of light on either side. The Faith has need for all truth.'

All Teilhard's being can be found in these wise words. He was to spend the rest of his life realizing their full meaning and implications.

## WITH EDWARD LE ROY

We cannot close this chapter of Père Teilhard's life without speaking of his close relations with that great philosopher, Edward Le Roy. In spite of the difference in age—Le Roy, who was born in 1870, was eleven years older than Teilhard—they had formed a genuine intellectual friendship. Every Wednesday there used to be gatherings at Le Roy's at which the great scientific, and especially biological, problems of the day were discussed.

Speaking on the occasion of his election to the Académie Française, M. Daniel-Rops recalled these discussions. It was the time at which Le Roy was working on his books, *Idealist Demands and the Fact of Evolution* (1927) and *Human Origins and the Evolution of Intelligence* (1928).[1] 'The two men', says Daniel-Rops, 'discussed so many of these problems that Edward Le Roy honestly admitted that he could no longer distinguish what came from him and what from his Jesuit friend.'

We should not only look in Le Roy's two books to find the precise meaning of the conclusions they both arrived at. We have very clear insight into them from the important article by Père Teilhard, published in Père Peillaube's *Revue de Philosophie* (1923), entitled 'Palaeontology and the appearance of Man'.

[1] Edward Le Roy's works were put on the *Index* on 1931. (Tr.)

The central idea of this work is summed up in the following phrase: 'The truth about Humanity today is that, starting from palaeontological data, there is only one way of understanding it. It (humanity) represents the end-product (privileged, if you wish) of the same biological process as that from which the whole tree of living things has grown.'

But he took care to note, as his conclusion, that biological Evolution does not explain everything in man. 'The secret of Man', he said, 'does not lie in the early stages of his embryonic (ontogenetic or phylogenetic) life which he has now passed beyond; it lies in the spiritual nature of his soul. But this soul which is a synthetic unity in action, escapes the grasp of Science, whose work is essentially that of analysing things in their elements and their material antecedents. Only intuition and philosophical reflection can discover it.'

## CHAPTER THREE

# In China

### THE GREAT ADVENTURE

WE have now reached the spring of 1923. Père Teilhard was forty-two. He held a professorship in the Institut Catholique of Paris, which had already been distinguished by A. de Lapparent (1839–1908), permanent secretary to the Academy of Sciences, and then by his son-in-law, Jean Boussac, born in 1885 and killed at the front, in 1916, a great specialist on nummulitids and cerithiids. Père Teilhard already had earned a considerable reputation in the scientific world, and a distinguished future was predicted for him. But it turned out to be not, as might have been expected, the career of a sedentary professor. We have already said that Teilhard had a passion for the ocean and for travel. No doubt it came from the vast horizons of the mountains which surrounded his childhood. During the war he once happened to be day-dreaming between two actions, and, as he wrote, 'If, shutting my eyes and slackening the reins of consciousness, I abandon my imagination to itself—let it follow its own old channels, its own recollections—I find vague memories arising in me of long journeys when I was a child. I see once more the moment when the different-coloured signals in the station light up to guide the great trains which seem to be urging their way towards a fascinating and magical future. Bit by bit the long line of signals, all illuminated, merge in my mind into a transcontinental railroad leading off into a limitless distance, somewhere beyond everything.'

And then he explained that his dream led him towards the East, where his 'projects for scientific discovery' took him. And he concluded 'That's what happened—I was caught. The enigmatic and tiresome "I" who so obstinately loves the front line, is exactly the same person, I can see, who loves adventure and research, who always wants to go off to the far ends of the world, to have new and unusual experiences and to be able to say he is ahead of everyone.'

This passage, which he called *Nostalgia for the Front* (September

1917), seems to have been a sort of premonition. At any rate the years that followed were a striking realization of the thoughts.

However strong his passion for travel, though, he had too much sense of discipline to yield to it without strong reasons. Père Licent, like him a Jesuit, had created a laboratory and museum for geological and palaeontological research in China. When an invitation came to Père Teilhard from there, he consulted his superiors—that is, we suppose, the Jesuit Provincial on the one hand and the Rector of the Institut Catholique on the other. Having been given the necessary authorization, he must surely have set off in great excitement and joy.

## IMPRESSIONS OF THE VOYAGE

Père Teilhard embarked at Marseille on April 6th, 1923. As far as Port Said he knew the landscape pretty well. From then on we shall follow his letters, collected and published by Mme Aragonnés. What these show us chiefly is not so much the expert as the poet, intoxicated with light, colours, reflections, scattered beauties. We cannot forbear to quote at least one example of this charming intoxication, and then have done. This is how he describes passing through the Suez Canal, in a letter of 15 April 1923:

'Sinai, a great block of granite and slashed red sandstone, and the Egyptian coast, at first regular and flat-lying, and then bristling with all sorts of extraordinary peaks, each of them equally raw and bare. Above them dreamlike tints, strangely soft in these extreme climates. To the East the sea seemed deep blue. Its horizon came to a sharp stop, clean like a knife blade. And then, above this dark band rose the mountains, without a break, a gentle pink, into a misty green sky. At sunset the West drew over itself all the beauty of the evening. As the sun gradually disappeared, in a little flurry of burning clouds, the mountains of Egypt, up till then hazy, began to pass through every shade of violet, from the deepest to the most transparent mauve. And a whole line of sharp points, like the teeth of a saw, were the last to be visible, standing out against the golden sky.'

You find passages like this scattered all over his private correspondence. But nearly always the poet gives way swiftly to the thinker, the scientist, the apostle, the visionary prophet that we shall find him to be. Mount Sinai which he looked at over there inevitably recalled his own history. 'I should have loved to visit those rocky slopes,' he wrote, 'not only to test them with my hammer, but also to listen and see if I could hear the voice from the Burning Bush. But has not the time passed when God speaks in the desert, and must we not understand now that "He Who Is" is not to be heard in this place or in that, for the summits where He dwells are not in inaccessible mountains, but in a profounder sphere of things? The secret of the world is everywhere where we manage to see the Universe as something transparent.'

However there is something which excites our traveller more than the changing colours of the countryside, more than the heavy opulence of the foliage and the flowers of Ceylon or even of Malaya, which he rates higher still; it is the sight and the study of human beings whom he meets and observes, from the negro in the stoke-hole or the Chinese servant, to the colonial administrator, the soldier, the merchant, and, in between them, the missionary. On the liner itself there was a whole floating universe. There he could measure what he calls 'the surface and the depths of the human stratum'. He had long talks with the ship's doctor and also with a colonial doctor. What astonished him, and would always astonish him, was the prodigious and poignant diversity of 'spirits'.

'Professors of theology', he wrote, 'would do well to pass through a stage such as I am going through at the moment. I begin to think that there is a particular view of the real world which is just as closed to some believers as the world of the Faith is to those who are not believers.' As an apostle of Christ it is clear that he was searching for something which he believed was absolutely essential, a common axis along which to orientate this diversity. 'It is the enormous mass of undisciplined human potentialities which gets me down,' he wrote on 11 May.

And after a long conversation with his ship's doctor and another passenger, he concluded sadly, 'We had finally to admit that we differed on points as fundamental as "Is it better to exist than not to exist?"' And then he adds, 'I think, in fact, that in all thought there is at this point a fundamental option, a postulate which is not demonstrable, but from which everything else is deduced. If one admits that being is better than its opposite, it is difficult to stop short of God. If one does not admit it, no further discussion is possible.'

All the rest of his life then, he feels that he will have to debate this problem: 'Is life absurd or is it divine?' That is the essential dilemma. Everything he wrote to his kinswoman in his first letters, he repeated in writing to the abbé Breuil from Tientsin, 25 May 1923:

'I should be rather nonplussed if I had to describe to you the precise state of my present inner feelings. The multitude of new things and persons I've seen the last two months, added to the uprooting from my own milieu, leaves me still in a sort of stupor. . . . For the moment I am chiefly dominated by the confused impression that the human world —to speak only of that—is an immense and disparate thing, just about as coherent, at the moment, as the surface of a choppy sea.'

And yet he cannot despair. He had a basic optimism which never flagged, for he continued: 'I still believe, for reasons coloured by mysticism and metaphysics, that this incoherence is only preparatory to a unification.'

We must not forget that the writer, as well as the recipient, of these lines were both well-known specialists in Palaeontology and Prehistory. They knew well how to pass outside the narrow framework of their scientific studies. These scholars were above all 'men' in the strong sense of that word; what is more, they were first and foremost priests. Of course Teilhard always kept his friend the abbé Breuil (who was four years his senior) in touch with his 'finds', first in Mongolia which he visited on trek, especially all along the Great Wall, on July 25th, 1923; and then to the frontiers of Chara-Ousso-Gol, in south-east Ordos —a bend in the Yellow River—the August 19th following. He lists with some pride, on this last date: 'Fifteen cases already (skeletons, or parts of them), a huge number of rhinoceros and gazelles, quite a few bisons (with enormous horns), strange wood-deer, horses, hemiones, a lamella of elephant (mammoth?) tooth, hyenas, wolves. It is a curious association. And man? Well, he must have been there, but here I must proceed methodically. . . . What is certain is that we now have two localities of palaeolithic date *in situ*, when three months ago none were known in China.'

But alongside this technical information, whether writing to the abbé Breuil or to his Aragonnés cousin, the religious note constantly creeps in. To the former, for instance, he writes: 'I have come to China to follow my star, and to steep myself in the sub-human zones of the universe.' (25 May.) 'I've never felt so distinctly, since my present isolation, how much you have become a profound and essential element in my life.' (16 July.) But it is above all in his letter of 26 August, alongside his account of his twenty-six large cases of fossils, that he expounds his thought in all its depth. We shall give the quotation a paragraph to itself.

## THE ONE THING NECESSARY

'I'm a bit too absorbed in Science', he says, 'to be able to philosophize much. But when I look into my heart I find myself more and more imbued with the inner conviction that the Science of Christ in all things, that is the true science of mysticism, is the only one that matters. I let myself get caught up again in the game when I geologize. But on the slightest reflection I see quite clearly that this occupation, though vital for me to the extent that it is a part of the whole trend of my life, by itself is of no final interest. As I pray, I gradually work out a bit better my "Mass upon Things". It seems to me that in a sense the true elements that have to be consecrated every day are the growth of the world that day: the bread symbolizing appropriately what Creation manages to produce, the wine (blood) what it loses, through exhaustion and suffering in its labour.'

These last lines summarize for us one of his writings, as yet unpublished, though it has circulated in cyclostyled copies; and it is an important part of Teilhard's production. We can thus date its composition to 1923, and it is called 'The Mass upon the World' (*La Messe sur le Monde*). Père Teilhard there shows himself preoccupied above all with giving his daily Mass a *cosmic function* and *planetary dimensions*. He comes to it by thinking of the consecrated Bread as the symbol of all effort and all the toil of humans at work, and the Wine as that of all suffering on earth. This, of course, he considered could be linked up with the most orthodox theology of the Holy Eucharist.

## HIS DEEPEST AIM

It is not only we who attribute to him this concern for the fullest orthodoxy. What he said to his friend the abbé Breuil, he said in other words to his cousin. In a letter from Sao-Kiao-Pan (south-east Ordos), of 12 September 1923, he summarized his method of work, on the one hand, and on the other his long-distance aims:

'Here in the North of Shen-si we have made some excellent collections: Jurassic plants, Miocene rhinoceros, and above all Palaeolithic implements at the very bottom of the loess. This last discovery, which completes and corroborates the two earlier ones (of Ning-Hia and of Chara-Ousso-Gol), is important and will make quite a stir in the world of Prehistory. I've sent word to Boule and Breuil, without forgetting Pekin. All in all, it seems to me that the good Lord has really led me by the hand this last three months. I now see in this Providential guidance a sign that He genuinely did want me to come out here, and also that He expects of me a renewed activity in my special apostolate in Europe: for *as you know, I only came to China in the hope of being better able to speak of "the mighty Christ" in Paris.* Indeed, I feel more and more strongly that *it is only this "mighty Christ" who can animate all my life.* But what a strange, sad thing life is, isn't it? We are led to admit that *the real stuff of the world is nothing which we touch, and that it is impossible for us to touch that which we then see to be the real stuff of the world.*'

We have italicized those words in the quotation which seem to us the essential ones. This opposition between what can be touched but is not the true reality, and that which cannot be touched but in which all reality can be found, seems to him to be the secret and the triumph of Faith; for he ends by quoting the words of the Gospel: *Beati qui non viderunt et crediderunt* ('Blessed are they that have not seen and yet have believed').

## INNER LIFE

We can be sure then that for him what counted most was the inner life, the progress of the soul, the ascent to God, the growth of divine love. Mme Aragonnés, summarizing many confidences she received from him in letters, well says that 'the "spiritualizing" value of the voyage was more important to him than its scientific interest, strong though that was'.

He wrote to her, in fact, from Tientsin, 15 October 1923: 'The voyage was over, and I felt keenly how little mere moving around in space adds, by itself, to man. When he gets back to where he started from, unless he has enlarged his inner life—a thing which can't be seen from outside anyway—he's just like anyone else.'

And in his diary, written on the 'heavy rectangular barge' which took him to Tientsin, he says specifically: 'What have I brought back from this four months' travel in Mongolia? Here, around me, in the bottom of the barge there are sixty cases piled up, full of fossils and stones. But they are all material things, external. In the innermost of my being. what have I gained during this long pilgrimage in China? What profound word has Greater Asia had to say to me?'

He had hoped to meet new currents of thought there, ancient wisdom, a mysticism which might rejuvenate and enrich our world of

Europe, which is losing itself in materialism. His hope was disappointed. 'For week after week', he wrote again in his diary, 'I was engulfed in the depth of the Asiatic masses. And now, as I try to collect my memories and impressions, I am bound to admit that in emerging from it, my search there too was fruitless. Nowhere among the men I met or about whom I was told did I see the smallest grain which might be destined to grow for the future life of mankind. Either *absence of thought, or senile thought or infantile thought*' (our italics) 'that's all I met during my voyage. . . . I haven't seen anything in Mongolia which awakened the "other life" in me. *I am a Pilgrim of the future, but I have come back from a voyage which was all in the past.*'

We should take special note of this last phrase. It shows us again the depth of someone like Teilhard. What interests him in Prehistory is not the curiosity to know what man was, but the secret of his future, the law of his evolution, the mystery of his final goal.

For he did believe in a final goal, since he believed in God and in Jesus Christ, since he believed in love. His journal at this point is quite emphatic: 'Sceptics, agnostics, false positivists, are wrong. Through the civilizations which replace each other, the World doesn't proceed at random, nor does it mark time, but beneath the universal movement of beings, something is being formed, no doubt something heavenly, but first something earthly. Nothing here below, none of man's travail, is lost to him. I believe that the only real science is the discovery of the growth of the universe, so I was distressed to have seen nothing during this voyage but traces of a vanished world. Why should I have been distressed? Surely the wake left behind by humanity in its progress shows us its movement just as clearly as the foam in front thrown up by the prow of other peoples' advance?'

He was so full of these thoughts that in a letter of 23 October from Tientsin, a letter of commiseration to the abbé Breuil on the death of his mother, he expressed himself thus: 'The further I travel in life, the more it seems to me that individual events should not count, but only our dedication to the future that is greater than us. I'm sure that your sorrow has merely thrown you even more resolutely into the great tasks which have become the deep interest of your life. . . . In addition, I try not to let slip my "interior life". The atmosphere of Paris doesn't help me from this point of view. I must admit that the journey in Mongolia did not directly give me any impetus in this respect: but indirectly it did anchor me in my faith in the Future. The World is only interesting looking forward: but from this angle it is thrilling.'

And his letter ended with a passage which betrays a moving friendship: 'I do so miss talking to you. Write to me. Goodbye, my dear man. I pray for you every day, commending to God those who are closest to me "in heart, in thought, in science". You belong to all three categories.'

## THE 1924 EXPEDITION

Père Teilhard returned to Tientsin on 13 October after his great research expedition in Ordos and Mongolia. He had at first planned to return to Europe in the autumn. But his exploration in 1923 had been so rich in realizations and in promises for the future that he decided to ask for an extension of leave from the Rector of the Institut Catholique and from Marcellin Boule, whose Museum was sponsoring his work, so as to be free in 1924 for a spring expedition. So he spent the winter partly at Tientsin, partly at Pekin. He mixed with the American and Chinese palaeontologists and geologists of Pekin. In November he wrote, 'I've seen nearly all the people of this category in China.' Dr. Granger particularly interested him—the palaeontologist of the great American expedition to Gobi. 'Here', he said, 'people chaff the Americans a good deal, but the more I see of them the more I admire their ability to take action and to get somewhere, and the more too I find them courteous and open-hearted towards me.'

And he adds this pertinent remark: 'This is one of the pieces of evidence which tend to make me savagely hostile to "accepted" judgements.' He grew deliberately less and less 'conformist', and was determined to judge by experience before reaching an opinion. This trait in his character needs emphasizing. So he saw many people, he observed, he weighed up every type of person, he established relationships which would follow him all his life, and he himself became 'international'.

As a good example of this he wrote from Pekin (8 January 1924) that 'The geological meeting was very lively. I made several new contacts there and learned a great deal, and much enjoyed the unreserved intimacy established between Chinese, Americans, Swedes, and Frenchmen. These new friendships were expressed in a continuous series of dinners.' One of these dinners was given by Dr. Ting, and Père Teilhard had 'a most interesting conversation with him on the intellectual condition of China'. Dr. Ting admitted that China was going through a religious crisis which he compared to that in France during the eighteenth century. 'The present phase', he said, 'is anti-religious. That will probably subside. But it remains true that the Chinese are by nature pragmatic and agnostic.'

However, Père Teilhard had not the faintest idea of the forthcoming passage of China into Marxist scientism. In February 1924 before setting off on his own research, he was glad also to make the acquaintance of Catholic Chinese and missionaries. He visited then the Mission at Che-li, south of Pekin, and its centre at Hsien-hsien. His impression is worth recalling for it is that of an anthropologist of the front rank. 'During the few days I spent there', he wrote (10 February), '. . . I felt what it must be like for missionaries to be plunged into the Chinese mass, an enormous, lifeless, earthy mass, instinctively hostile to foreigners who have come to suggest changes for which they have not the slightest desire.' And we get the same note at the end of a second journey about six hundred miles from Pekin, on the borders of Che-li and Ho-Nan: 'I have been from one kind of Christianity to another, and I have seen at close hand what the missionary's life is like, no longer in large houses but out in the bush. So I've been able to verify what people have told me: the greatest test for the missionary in China is to find himself immersed in a sea of primitive human beings, good and affectionate, no doubt, but inquisitive, clinging, indiscreet, like savages. . . . Among the Chinese, and still more as between Chinese and Europeans, the conventional and the rough approximation hold sway. Thus one has the impression of living in a fluid, elusive milieu.'

But at last spring came, and the expedition by caravan towards the Gobi was under way. Unfortunately the results were not as fruitful as he had hoped. There was plenty that was picturesque, but he was not travelling as a tourist. He wrote on the bank of the Shiling-Gol (2 June), 'So far I seem to have lost the gambit (from the palaeontological point of view). From the geological point of view I think I have done some genuine work, but that wasn't exactly what Boule and I had hoped from this expedition.'

Eight days later, still in the Gobi, he announced that he had found his first fossils: but a poor haul so far. About the 25th of June he was a bit more satisfied: 'We've made some progress the last two weeks,' he said. '. . . This last stage has been satisfying from a palaeontological point of view. . . . What's more, all along the Dalai-Nor and to the west, over more than sixty miles I was surprised to discover a chain of quaternary volcanoes, as fresh as our peaks in the Auvergne.' He must have been delighted to find his favourite 'peaks' from his childhood days so far from his homeland: or rather to discover them, for 'I wonder whether anybody has ever spotted them: I rather suspect not', he said proudly.

The expedition came to an end without any other important results.

However he noted that he was returning from the Far East with a conviction deeper than ever that 'without knowledge and without research there can be no further human developments nor a true mysticism today'. Perhaps this is an exaggeration: but he explains it thus—'I am so fully and so rationally convinced of the spiritual value of the urge towards consciousness, the very sap of the tree of life of which our privileged species occupies the summit.'

This thought is and always will be the essence of his book, *Le Phénomène humain*, which was already beginning to be formed in his mind.

On the 10th September 1924, Père Teilhard went to Shanghai to meditate at the tomb of his older sister who died in 1911 at thirty-three as Superior of the Little Sisters of the Poor in this town. Then he set off for France.

## A FRESH DEPARTURE IN 1926

Père Teilhard may have thought that his return to France would see him settled down for good in Paris. A tremendous amount of activity was planned for him both in the scientific and in the religious field. The Museum wanted to annex him. But he preferred to keep his teaching at the Institut Catholique. There he was in touch with the intellectual élite, first his students, and also the young folk from the great schools, those of the Social Union of Catholic Engineers, and the 'Talas'[1] or Catholic students of the École Normale Supérieure.

What happened then is difficult to ascertain precisely but the general situation is easy enough to guess. Teilhard was a forerunner. He had already travelled over the globe and meditated in the wide open spaces. His vision of things had become 'cosmic'. His resulting views were highly personal, accepted by some with enthusiasm while others were shocked at them; and soon his Jesuit superiors were frightened. He himself simply went straight ahead neither provoking nor refusing discussion.

Finally it was decided that he should limit himself to the scientific domain and, to do so, return to China. Père Teilhard was used to seeing the will of God and the call of Providence everywhere, and so he accepted. Nothing would ever set him up against his lawful superiors. But the experience, as he said himself, gave him the feeling of 'growing old'. On April 26th, 1926, en route for China which he had never hoped to see again, he wrote privately to his sister:

[1] Tr.: From the popular greeting 'Va-t'-à la messe?'

'For the third time since 1906 I am passing Bonifacio. . . . I've certainly aged, even during the last three years, even the last eighteen months. Ideas don't spring up in me with the same exuberance, the same perennial intoxication as they used to do. This prolific fertility only lasts for a time in any one human life.' But he added at once: 'On the other hand I don't think I've changed fundamentally. Though with less warmth and almost without enthusiasm it is still the same kind of grasp of the world that I am looking for.'

And once more on the steamer, the *Angkor*, he experienced the same diversity of human beings. 'The more I globe-trot,' he said, 'the more aware I am of the richness and variety of the lives and temperaments which we want to force into one mould.' And that sets the Christian apostle the most difficult problems. 'What an enormous thing the world is for a religion to have to assimilate! This strikes me more than it did the last time, as I traverse these exotic peoples: one seems to come up against watertight compartments between minds, and one has got to dive deep underneath them to establish any real communication between souls and to "convert" them. "Conversion" seems to me a problem which is more and more difficult to understand.'

That was what led him to the desire to enlarge contemporary apologetic methods, an idea which in any case he had had for a long time, but which became stronger as he met men of his scientific culture. The following quotation, of 19 June 1926, is very revealing in this connection:

'The day before yesterday a very friendly professor from Harvard addressed a Sino-American audience and told us, very simply and humbly, how he understood the awakening of thought in the animal series. I thought of the abyss which separates the intellectual world I was in and whose language I understand, from the theological and Roman world whose idiom I also know. After a first shock at the thought that the latter may and must be as real as the former, I said to myself that now I was perhaps in a position, while speaking the first language, to give a genuine explanation of what the second preserves and repeats in its language, which has become incomprehensible to so many.' This was going henceforth to be the supreme aim of his life, the reconciliation of science and faith.

And he noted, in a great act of faith and hope: 'However bizarre it may seem at first, I ended by realizing that here and now Christ is not a stranger to Professor Parker's preoccupations, and that with the aid of certain connecting links it would be possible to get him to pass from his positivist psychology to a kind of mystical perspective. This fact reassured me.' And with a great leap of the heart he ended: 'Here are the Indies which draw me more than those which drew St. Francis Xavier. But here too are enormous problems, not of rites but of ideas, to be resolved before we can truly convert them.'

## THE DIVINE MILIEU

From now on he pursued the aims which we have just seen him revealing. His work in palaeontology, though still very exciting to him, was in his view only an opening upon the souls of his contemporaries and, as he was soon to say, a platform or a pulpit from which he could preach Christ. The first stage to be covered was, he believed, to get rid of particularities that paralyse development. As he wrote on 1 September 1926, 'I wanted to expound the psychology, the mixed feelings of pride, hope, deception and expectation of man who sees himself no longer as French or Chinese but as terrestrial.' Man can never be regrouped unless the barriers are broken down. Père Teilhard does not mention the Iron Curtain, which may seem surprising, nor does he foresee the Bamboo Curtain. Or if he does think of it, he sees it only as another false step to be corrected. However he has a slight scruple about it, for he says in the same passage to his cousin, 'You know of course that these feelings have nothing anti-Christian about them; on the contrary, I believe that they call for the unique manifestation of a still greater Christ.'

It was then that, on the 7th November after rounding off a considerable piece of palaeontological work, he envisaged the publication of a book which would expound his fundamental ideas. 'I have decided', he says, 'to write my devotional book: to draw up as simply as possible the ascetic or mystical doctrine which I have been living and preaching for such a long time. I call it *Le Milieu divin*, but I'm being careful to see that nothing esoteric and a minimum of explicit philosophy gets into it. My aim is not to go outside the realm of a moral attitude which will be in its strength compatible with an incontestably Christian outlook. I really want to "make the grade" and to get myself read. I fancy that if I can get my work printed there'll be a double advantage: first to spread around ideas which I believe will liberate many minds; and next, to get a sort of approval of the Church for my effort.' 'I've set to upon my little book,' he adds, 'and I'd like to write it slowly, calmly, living it and meditating on it, like a prayer.'

The book was written at Tientsin, in November 1926, to convey one of his deepest personal experiences. It is difficult to summarize briefly. Perhaps it is enough to appeal to the words of St. Paul, speaking of God before the Areopagus: 'In Him we live and move and have our being.' But every being, from the most humble upwards, can say as much. The *Divine Milieu* is God Himself considered as being the milieu in which all things, from one end of the Cosmos to the other, live and move, and have their being. A poet has said 'Tread softly: all the earth is sacred.' But we must not think of Père Teilhard's thought as a sort of pantheism. On the contrary, what he says is profoundly Christian. The equivalent could be found in St. John of the Cross and all the great mystics. It is quite simply the dogma of the omnipresence of God. It is the translation of St. Paul's phrase concerning Christ: 'He is the image of the invisible God, the firstborn of every creature: For by him were all things created, that are in heaven, and that are in earth, visible and invisible, whether they be thrones, or dominions, or principalities, or powers: all things were created by him, and for him: And he is before all things, and by him all things consist.' (Col. i. 15–17.)

Père Teilhard's *Le Milieu divin* was completed in March 1927. It was sent to one of his friends at Louvain and he received enthusiastic approval from him. A professor of theology at Louvain said: 'These pages seem to me superb, magisterial. I think they are original, highly novel, and yet as authentically traditional as possible. . . . I hope they will be published as soon as they can.'

In spite of everything the discussions that went on with a view to their publication were fruitless. 'This work is still unpublished', said Mme Aragonnés.[1] Only cyclostyled copies of it circulated, as of many othei writings of Père Teilhard, such as 'How I Believe' (*Comment je crois*, 1934), 'Human Energy' (*L'Énergie humaine*, 1937), 'The Spirit of the Earth' (*L'Esprit de la Terre*, 1931), 'Sketch of a Personal Universe' (*Esquisse d'un Univers personnel*, 1936), 'Some Reflections on the Conversion of the World' (*Quelques réflexions su la Conversion du Monde*, 1936), 'Let us Save Humanity' (*Sauvons l'Humanité*, 1936), and 'The Spiritual Phenomenon' (*Le Phénomène spirituel*, 1937), which we mention here *en bloc* so as not to have to come back to them. And there will be many others between 1942 and 1954.

But in February 1927 a new stage in his scientific activity opened up which we must discuss in the following chapter.

[1] It forms vol. IV of the Collected works published by Éditions du Seuil. 1957 (Tr.)

## CHAPTER FOUR

# Towards the Discovery of *Sinanthropus*

### HIS POWERS WIDENED

As we know already it was the Paris Museum which met the expenses of Père Teilhard's researches. The means at his disposal were naturally rather limited. So when in February 1927 Père Teilhard was offered by the Carnegie Foundation the supervision of work on the study of vertebrates and of Man in China, in collaboration with Chinese, Swedish and American specialists, he did not hesitate to accept, in spite of the hesitations and repugnance of his old teacher, Marcellin Boule. Rather than argue with him he promised to let him see the results. The organization which was now formed in Pekin included several centres: the *Geological Survey* (Chinese-American-Swedish), the *Rockefeller Medical Institute* (American-Chinese), the *Free Chinese University* (an American foundation), the *Geological Society* and the *Natural History Society*, a regrouping of the same experts as in the preceding centres, and finally the *Institute for Prehistoric Research*, supported by the Carnegie Foundation. There was an atmosphere of frank cordiality among all the scientists in Pekin, and it was precisely this possibility of 'meeting' between minds from all points of the globe which evoked the vast hopes of Père Teilhard: for he regarded himself as a sort of missionary or Catholic Chaplain to the world of science, appointed by Providence to rally all the world, first of all on the human plane, and then on the Christian—'above all national, racial, and even "confessional" barriers' as he wrote (20 February 1927). And Mme Aragonnés notes in this context: 'The idea often recurs in his letters that his authority as a man of science can assure him of an audience among unbelievers or believers, and at the same time that his religious loyalty is the best witness.' He says more explicitly himself: 'It is my view of the world and of Christ which is put to the test in my life itself.' That is all that he thinks of in all his work. On the 11th June 1927, right in the middle of his research, he writes: 'It is the Other I am pursuing, the

Thing right through on the other side. . . .' And the same letter tells us that 'My most active moment of the day is still the one when I say my "Mass upon the World", to divinize the day that is beginning.'

We know already what he means by his 'Mass upon the World': it enabled him to offer to the Creator, under the species of Bread all human effort, and under that of Wine all human suffering. We have quite a long passage of his, dating from 1923, in which he expounds his feeling. If we did not know for sure from other contexts that he repudiated all kinds of pantheism, this passage might seem here and there to be difficult to dissociate from a certain disturbing flavour of monism. But in his private reflections we often have what are largely poetic expressions which it would be foolish and unfair to press for a literal meaning.

Such lines as the following, as we shall see when we come to them in their right context, should be interpreted in the light of his teaching as a whole:

'Thou glorified Christ, an Influence which spreads unseen at the heart of Matter, and a dazzling centre at which the countless threads of the Multiple come together. Thou whose brow is of snow, whose eyes are of fire, whose feet sparkle more than molten gold; Thou whose hands imprison the stars, Thou who art the first and the last, the living, the dead, the risen again; Thou who dost sum up in thine overwhelming unity every delight, every taste, every power, every state. My longing for You is as wide as the Universe, and so it is to You my whole being appeals: Thou are truly my Lord and my God. . . . Thy creative attraction has found many new well-springs in me: by these, and by my knowledge, however feeble, by my religious ties, by my priesthood, and (which is what I most cling to) by the depth of my human conviction—by all these I offer myself to Your heart, that heart which covers all, I vow it for life and death, Jesus.'

These are, one must admit, unforgettable accents. His 'Mass upon the World' was undoubtedly the most effective means for the *cosmic* action which he believed he was appointed to perform on this earth.

One cannot help, though, having a few doubts when we find him affirming, as in his letter of 4 July 1927, that 'does not the Spirit animate all things, even plants, even stones?' *Animate* stones? That does not seem to make sense at all. It will be one of the things we shall have to examine later on. We find what seems to be the same idea in a letter of 7 August 1927, in which he says 'Though I haven't had much time to think, the last three months, on the other hand my ideas have settled down and become clearer, so that the important elements in them now take their proper place. And so I can now see more clearly how much my inner life is finally dominated by these twin mountains: a limitless faith in Our Lord, animator of the World, and a quite distinct faith in the world (especially the human world) animated by God. *Opportune et importune*,[1] as St. Paul says, I feel myself bound to declare myself a "believer" in the future of the World, in spite of appearances, in spite of a false orthodoxy which confuses progress with materialism, change with liberalism, the perfecting of man with naturalism.'

This last sentence must have been one of those which made his Jesuit superiors in Paris cock their ears. However he ended the passage with astonishing assurance: 'My sole ambition is to leave behind me the marks of a logical life directed wholly towards the World's great hopes. There lies the future of man's religious life. I am as sure of this as I am of my own existence.'

It is clear from this letter that Père Teilhard believed that he was charged with a sort of 'cosmic' mission, to light up the future of all humanity through a scientific knowledge of his most distant past. He entered more and more deeply into this rôle which Providence seemed to have assigned to him. And it is only in this vast perspective that we can understand him at all. At the moment what he had to do was to enlarge his qualifications in the scientific sphere. And that is how he moved, without knowing it, along the road towards the sensational discovery with which his name will always be linked: that of *Sinanthropus.*

## TOWARDS *Sinanthropus*

Père Teilhard left for France on 27 August 1927, and stayed there for a year. On 7 November 1928, he set off again for the Far East. On the way he was amicably detained in Ethiopia by Henri de Monfreid, for a geological and palaeontological exploration of that country. This meant new contacts for him with an unknown world, with picturesque and backward native inhabitants. About them he wrote from Dire-Daoua, on December 28th, 'It would be fascinating to know about their habits and customs, but I have grave doubts that they will ever form part of the advance wing of humanity.' And he wrote to Max and Simone Bégouën, on 8 January 1929, about the same people, that 'They are a fine type of humanity surviving here, but very unsuited to follow our forward march. They'll just melt away or disappear, like zebras and elephants. J * * * will say that I'm exclusive and

[1] In season and out of season.

fierce; but honestly, the more I look and the more I think, the more I can see no other way out for thought and action than an obscure faith in the march of Thought (or of Spirit, if you like), which is an insatiable power and destroys everything that has had its time. This physical reality of Thought, which eclipses (or rather restores to itself) all the mightiest properties that have been attributed to Matter during a century of research, more and more tends to dominate my outlook.'

And when he set off once more for China, after having found the basis for 'at least two nice little memoirs on Ethiopia and Somaliland', on the liner, he fell to pondering, with an agility and freshness of mind which he was delighted to note, that 'There only truly exists for me now one World of Spirit—but not a metaphysical Spirit, in the manner of Hegel, I imagine. The Spirit I think I can detect is charged with the remnants of Matter. All the greatness, all the physical and historical attributes which science has for a hundred and fifty years assigned to the latter, I can see transferred to a particular "stuff" of things. For me Entropy has been replaced by "the highest consciousness" as the essential physical function of the Cosmos. If I dare put it this way, the World seems to me to have "stumbled" forward and upward upon the spiritual, and this inversion of Cosmogony results in giving a cosmic consistency to the centres of consciousness, the Monads: and so the individual richness of souls is something imperishable, and the supreme Centre must be something both lovable and loving.'

We should remember this outline carefully: all its elements will be found in Père Teilhard's final synthesis, expounded in *Le Phénomène humain*.

Finally he got back to China. In his absence vital discoveries had been made, in December 1928, in the caves of Chou-Kou-Tien, about thirty miles from Pekin. They all concerned *Sinanthropus*, and this date is important in Prehistory. Père Teilhard was appointed to supervise the finished work in this category, in China, and he saw in it one of the greatest opportunities in his whole scientific career. He was more than ever convinced that, as he said, 'the mystic pulse is inseparable from the scientific pulse and needs equally to be given a chance'. That was to be his job. He threw himself into the tasks which this scientific mission involved. He 'went over to the Chinese' as he puts it, so that the mission should produce its maximum. He mixed with the Chinese, he almost became one of them, and wanted above all to avoid the reefs of Chinese xenophobia. And he succeeded strikingly. He was invited by Dr. Ting to come to Chou-Kou-Tien and he accepted at once. The exact part he played in the *Sinanthropus* affair can be seen in this passage from a letter written from Tientsin 6 May 1929: 'The supervision of Chou-Kou-Tien is much too important a work for me to think of refusing. . . . A little Ford took me and my two companions, along impossible roads, to the village near the excavations. And, well, in the end I am highly satisfied with it all. First, from the technical point of view, I think I managed to throw a little more light on the history of the henceforward very famous stratum. And next, I was very touched with the good will and the respect paid to me by my new pupils.'

And yet in spite of all that, it was not here that he saw his main task to lie, at this moment. For he ends, 'This first attempt gives me courage for the trip up the Shan-si, which will no doubt be much more interesting to me and my companion than the unprofitable work we've just finished.'

And so he and his companion, Père Émile Licent, organized a voyage into Manchuria in May 1929, which would teach him 'an enormous amount about the ancient and recent geology and the Prehistory of this country'. He returned to Tientsin on 10 June, but set off again on 6 July for Shen-si, and from there on to Shan-si. From July onwards he notes 'important observations touching the geology of Hwang-Ho, which turns out to be probably Palaeolithic, and extends my finds of 1923 by several hundred kilometres'.

And all the time he does not forget, among his scientific studies, the great syntheses which he is constructing in his mind. A letter written from Tai-Yuan, on the Shan-si, 16 September, shows this: '. . . I am thinking of a third and much fuller version of the *Mass upon the World*—a project I haven't realized yet—and also of an essay on *The Physics of the Mind*, in which I shall try to show (as I think I see it) that Science is now forced, especially since the notion of Evolution and Time (*la Durée*) has invaded even the physics of Matter, to build its explanations of the empirical world upon Mind. That will lead me to present all in one, a sort of spiritual Cosmogony (but not a metaphysic) of *the person*. Taken obliquely it seems to me that the immortality of the soul and of Personality (the Super-Personality of God) ceases to be an interested or an anthropomorphic truth, and takes on an essential significance in the structure of the World. I want to try to get that down, at least in a rough draft.' This is what he did later in an essay entitled 'Sketch of a Personal Universe' (*Esquisse d'un Univers personnel*, 1936).

During this time the excavations which he had instigated at Chou-Kou-Tien went on without him and had obtained results which he said he was most 'excited' about. And he listed them: 'Jawbones and fragments of skull of a very strange anthropoid or hominid; the dentition is entirely human, the shape of the jaw typically simian, cranium of quite human dimensions (?). If this last point is confirmed (the pieces are not yet completely disentangled) that is the *coup de grâce* to the adversaries of Transformism extended to Man.'

## NEW PROBLEMS

This last sentence of his letter shows the very serious problem which he sees will be posed to Science and to himself. On November 11th, 1929, he wrote to Max Bégouën from Tientsin: 'With a Chinese I have prepared . . . the first geological and palaeontological report yet made on the famous *Sinanthropus* stratum at Chou-Kou-Tien. All this is very exciting.' But he also prepared an important article on the *Sinanthropus* for the Paris public, which he dated from Pekin, April 1930, and which was published in the *Revue des Questions scientifiques* of 20 July 1930. In this article (recently republished in vol. II of his *Works*), he recalled in rough outline the history of the excavations at Chou-Kou-Tien, begun in 1922 and ending in 1929, with about fifteen hundred cases of different kinds of fossils, including the famous *Sinanthropus*.

On this topic he notes that 'The preparation and the study of the remains of *Sinanthropus* fell entirely upon Dr. Davidson Black, who completed this double task with consummate skill and expertise.' But his conclusion is of capital importance:

'From a more general point of view it will be obvious to all that the discovery of *Sinanthropus* represents a serious victory won by the upholders of the extension of Transformism to the human zoological form. This success is likely to have certain troublesome consequences, even for true Science. Many affirmations which have an old-fashioned materialist smell about them, already have been and certainly will be still more trotted out with reference to "Pekin Man".'

That in his view is the real problem. And he has his answer ready: that it is not by the embryo that we can judge of the adult being. How could one guess the oak from the acorn from which it springs? The same is true of man, of all humanity:

'This is the moment to insist that no consideration drawn from palaeontology can ever detract from the astonishing grandeur of the *present human fact*. Human palaeontology labours only, in fact, to discover the embryo-genesis of the human species. But embryonic states cannot enable one to define the value of the adult being in the case of Man as species any more than in the case of Man as individual.'

And then he indicates the interest of Prehistory thus: 'The *Sinanthropus* helps us very conveniently to understand better what are the successive stages of appearance by which the human type has been able to form in the midst of all the rest of living things. But for even a scientific appreciation of the prodigious event which the appearance of Thought represents in the history of the Earth, we have to look in another direction. The scientific solution of the problem of man cannot be determined by the study of fossils, but by a more careful consideration of the properties and possibilities in Man today which enable one to predict the Man of tomorrow.'

Further, in a second article in the same review in 1934, he recalls opportunely that 'the traces of the Past which Science discovers for us are only *a shadow* of what really existed'. It would therefore be ridiculous to draw extreme conclusions from sporadic remains and from the 'evidences of a vast layer which, at a particular moment, covered everything'. For himself, he did not feel he could pronounce dogmatically upon the degree of 'humanity' of *Sinanthropus*.

In the meanwhile he had managed to visit Paris, and the abbé Breuil, who narrates the principal theme of their conversation thus: 'I remember Père Teilhard coming to my office at the Institute of Prehistory during the winter of 1930, putting down on my desk a little stag's horn, peduncle and all, and saying: "I shan't tell you where this comes from: but what do you make of this object?"—I replied: "That it has been put in the fire when still fresh; that it is an instrument fashioned by man in sharpening the remains of the frontal-bone by percussion with a stone implement, the marks of which you can see on the shaft of the peduncle."—"But", he said, "it comes from Chou-Kou-Tien!"—"It doesn't matter where it comes from," I replied, "I still maintain my diagnosis."'

And the abbé Breuil thought the matter so important that he wanted to visit Chou-Kou-Tien to see the things *in situ*. He did go there, in fact, in the autumn of 1931, but did not find Père Teilhard there, as the latter had already set off on the 'Yellow Expedition', which we shall discuss below. The abbé Breuil persisted in his judgement, but Père Teilhard continued doubtful. In his second article on *Sinanthropus*, written in 1934, he said, 'The existence of an instrument of bone, admitted by my friend Professor H. Breuil, remains in my own opinion problematic. Many pieces are striated or broken artificially: but the evidence of a systematic use of bones or of stag's horn is still inconclusive.' The abbé Breuil, on the other hand, said of him in his article in *La Table Ronde*, June 1955, 'To my great regret he never emerged from his original reserve on the subject. That is because Teilhard, though wonderfully observant of the terrain in geology, and an admirable palaeontologist, never became expert in the study of prehistoric technique, and the marks of industry partly escaped him.'

### THE YELLOW EXPEDITION[1]

Père Teilhard, known from now on all over the world, had given his support in principle to the organizers of the Yellow Expedition which had been in preparation since 1929. So he returned to France in September 1930, to make contact with the bold explorers in this 'raid' organized by the Citroën mission. He was appointed by this mission to go to the U.S.A. to negotiate on various important matters. He had in fact some friends in New York whom he had known well in China, especially Henry Fairfield Osborn and Roy Chapman Andrews of the New York Museum of Natural History. He was sad to observe, when he mixed in American religious circles, that to the Catholics there Evolution was still synonymous with materialist monism. He was to spend the rest of his life combating this prejudice. 'Anyway,' he wrote, 'in Paris they see things more subtly.' He thought of men like Lapparent, Termier, the abbé Breuil and so many others, who admitted the fact of Evolution without seeing in it any blow to their religious certitudes. One of his joys in New York was to meet Claudel, though he regarded him as a great poet who was so sure of his Christianity and his biblical outlook that he couldn't comprehend even the possibility of a valid objection from the side of scientific discovery. That was all the more reason for him, Teilhard, to survey this sector of the front in human thought, since he knew and could measure its importance so much better. And that was why he was so pleased to have the 'delightful' welcome he received from Osborn, Andrews and the others. Osborn especially, who was the Director of the Museum, declared him 'the adopted son of the house'.

After that he returned to China by the Pacific Ocean, on the *President Garfield*, a small but comfortable ship, to take part in the Yellow Expedition. In the spring of 1931 he was back in Pekin. The first aim of the Yellow Expedition was to demonstrate how the Citroën caterpillar-wheels could eat up any obstacle in the Asiatic deserts. The departure of the Chinese group, who were to meet the group coming from the Near East at Kashgar, in Turkestan, was fixed for early April.

[1] Croisière Jaune.

## RESULTS

It does not fall within our ambit to tell about this enormous voyage, punctuated with so many incidents, sometimes mechanical, sometimes diplomatic and political. But we must indicate its results briefly. As we can guess from what we know of Père Teilhard, its first result in his eyes was to enlarge his knowledge of men. He talked to his companions on the journey, he saw new people: he reflected, observed, compared. And on May 4th, 1931, he wrote: 'I was struck with the difficulty there is in getting certain universalistic perspectives understood at all by men who have never been Christians, or who have at bottom escaped all Christian influence—for Christianity shows itself as the only spiritual force which is capable of developing in men's hearts the sense of the Absolute and the Universal, above all in a personal version, that is to say the real "mystical sense".' And his reflections along this line ended up in the essay of 1936, called 'Sketch of a Personal Universe' (*Esquisse d'un Univers personnel*). That was one more step towards the formulation of his greatest work, *Le Phénomène humain*.

Another result of this fine expedition he gives in the following lines, written on December 21st, 1931, on his return journey and, as he says, 'on the slopes of Pekin': 'Breuil must have reached Pekin at the end of October, just at the right moment to appreciate and criticize the discovery of implements, which I set in hand the previous April. And I wasn't there to meet my old friend whom I myself brought out!' But in a letter written a little earlier he summed it all up: 'The inconveniences of a thing are part of the thing itself. In the end I have almost doubled my knowledge of Asia. Ten months of life, even at fifty, are not too much to pay for that.'

On his return he learned at Pekin of the death of his father, on February 11th, 1932. A series of family bereavements, all of them touching his heart very near, were to follow, although he was so far away from all of them. With his sensitive and affectionate nature this was one of the most painful tests imposed by the necessities of his scientific career. He was never able to be at the bedside of his relatives, even when he knew that they were near death, nor could he join his brothers and sisters in the mourning which affected them all profoundly.

## A TURNING-POINT IN HIS LIFE

It was during this same year 1932 that he felt the impression of having reached the main turning-point of his life. The Yellow Expedition had ended in March. The heroes of the expedition had been fêted in Pekin, but for the rest of the journey all the plans made were upset by the death of M. Haardt, one of the leaders of the adventure, after a short illness. Père Teilhard was very shocked, and wrote from Pekin on March 18th: 'Personally the sudden disappearance of a man whose heart and affection had endeared me to him, was a great grief to me.' And at once the priest in him—that is to say the 'hunter of souls' (the title given to St. Gaétan of Thyana)—added 'a grief which was all the greater because I could not be there at the last moment. As I know Haardt, I think he would have leaned on me at that moment, and I am sure I could have smoothed the way for him. That is my real sorrow.

A bit later Père Teilhard had to undergo a period of extreme exhaustion of both body and soul. This was because a journey to the Shan-si seemed necessary for his research, and yet it seemed hard to have to set off again less than two months after the interminable expedition. He wrote (11 July 1932) from Taiyuan, on the Shan-si: 'En route again, since July 4th. Once more, long journeys by mule, dirty inns, flies.... This seemed to me very tough, from the point of view of morale, at first. I don't know why I felt myself so low at the end of June: physical tiredness partly, turning into moral disgust. Still, with the help of the interest of the research itself, I feel that the journey will go all right.' But why this new effort? We must not think that his reasons for it were purely mundane: 'I had a sense', he wrote, 'that I ought to make this new attempt if I wanted to be faithful to what God asks of me.' However, he did feel that he would have to change his methods somewhat, for he went on: '. . . But I fancy that this is the last time that I shall travel round in this way. I can foresee new perspectives now, but probably of a different kind and more suitable to my age and to the kind of work I can contribute now. In every way I believe that I am reaching a turning-point in my life. And it is precisely so as not to miss this turning-point that I have undertaken this present journey.'

If we understand these words properly, and above all if we consider the rest of Père Teilhard's life, this turning-point in his life will appear in a twofold aspect, which the following chapters of this book will aim at describing. On one side, he is going to become a sort of 'international expert' on the subject of Prehistory, so much so that nothing will happen in this realm without him, like his friend the abbé Breuil, being invited to go to the spot to see what it is all about. And on the other side, he is going to bring to fruition his great work, *Le Phénomène humain*, which will be his message to the world, the last testament of his thinking—already the elements of it were there together in his mind. And he reckoned that his book would have a reception in scientific circles—which was what he was aiming at—the more favourable the more his quality as an expert was obvious. These two things lay close together, in his deepest convictions. By force of circumstance he had to remain a great traveller; but from now on he would take part in large expeditions organized by powerful scientific foundations. As a result it was all going to be easier for him, not so rough on his gradually declining powers, and also more effective.

CHAPTER FIVE

# The International Expert on Prehistory

## A FRESH VOYAGE IN CHINA

AFTER his journey to the Shan-si Père Teilhard had managed to return to France for a brief stay of about four months, from September 1932 to January 1933. And then back he went to China, which was still for a time his special domain. It was there that he was soon to receive American invitations for his later surveys. And at this date China was threatened with war. In the course of his voyage he first travelled with the abbé Breuil, who came to Abyssinia to meet Monfreid there. And then he was able to use the long leisure of the trip on the *Aramis* in working alone in his cabin, which was airy and roomy. He wrote to Max Bégouën on 6 March 1933 that 'I seized the opportunity to set down in a few pages, with the title "The Structure of the Spirit" (*La Structure de l'Esprit*), a few ideas which seem to me to have come out of our conversations during the autumn.' We can see that his thought was always developing: his work was getting ready bit by bit. And in the same letter he confronted the troubles which he was going to meet in China, and wrote: 'Is it still going to be possible to work? This is the time to cling hard to one's destiny, or if you like, to the hand of God, so as not to miss the invitation that comes from things.'

This is the language of a man who, as we have already seen, believed intensely in divine Providence. Nothing happens without His permission and the call of God can be found in every event that awaits us.

On March 24th, 1933, he arrived at Pekin. 'The end of the voyage was not much fun,' he wrote on the 26th: 'the ship was empty; we were travelling up into the cold. . . .' In the Chinese capital he found the situation uncertain. The country was divided. They were expecting the Japanese to seize the town. 'The collections in the Museum have been put in cases,' he said, 'and sent up to the Shanghai concessions.' A month later he was still there, amidst the sounds of war which could be heard about one hundred and fifty miles higher up—'for form's sake', as he says. The Survey of which he was the director had removed its collections. A good number, however, remained at the Rockefeller Foundation at Pekin, with his friend Dr. Davidson Black, a prehistorian of great distinction, with whom he worked closely.

Two months later, on June 10th, he wrote that 'Pekin has been through a very feverish week'. Then everything grew calm again, as if enchanted. An agreement, of which the clauses were not known, had been reached between Japanese and Chinese. There was a fresh removal of books and collections, to bring the Survey together again. He profited by this relaxation to make a swift tour—a 'trip' he called it—to the Shan-si with an American friend. And then came the change in his life, of which he had a foreboding. They were expecting him in New York to submit to his examination some fossils from China and Mongolia, destined for the City Museum. So it was, as we have said, a survey which was entrusted to him: and once caught in these toils he never got out of them.

## TO WASHINGTON

At first sight he was not very enamoured of what was offered him. In the letter of 10 June already quoted he says why: 'Now I am getting ready for my departure to Washington. I am to leave Pekin on the 22nd and Shanghai on the 27th. The Congress is from July 20th to 30th; then a trip to the West. I think I shall re-embark at San Francisco on September 15th. I'm not wildly excited about this new voyage, because it seems to me so much time taken away from my personal research, of which I grow more jealous as I grow older; but it may open unseen horizons or relationships for me. I can't miss this chance.' We note that there is no trace of personal ambition in his attitude, but the steady desire to be always ready to follow the designs of God upon him.

So he made the voyage to Washington, aboard the luxurious American liner, *President Coolidge*. At New York he found many old friends at the Museum. He did the job they wanted him to do. He next went to the Congress of Prehistory at Washington, and there presented a book entitled "Fossil Man in China" (*L'Homme Fossile en Chine*). He also submitted a communication to the Congress, lunched at the French embassy, then set off for San Francisco so as to return to China. But on the way he took part in a geologists' excursion in Sierra Nevada and the Grand Canyon. He was enchanted with everything he saw, and he wrote from California on 11 September: 'In addition to the excursion to Sierra Nevada, I spent three days touring in the South, about a thousand miles, as far as Santa Barbara, with Camp—an American colleague—and three of his pupils. Fascinating geology, and a most attractive country. I am very fond indeed of these wild and sunlit mountains, covered with green oak and laurel trees, or with cactus and yuccas. And also, life is so simple, so *un-conventional*! [sic in original]. You sleep outside, eat at any old time, at a bar, squatting on a high stool. No one bothers about you if you want to be quiet. After a month's stay I feel quite at home in California.'

And indeed he met friends everywhere, or made new ones. He studied geology in a wonderful setting. As he says again, he 'sniffed the odour of forests and sequoias'. His general impression was very favourable. 'America', he wrote to Max and Simone Bégouën, 'is a country of freshness and expansion. I really breathed an air there which is missing in France.'

## *Sinanthropus* AGAIN

After this long detour, which seemed like a parenthesis but was, unknown to him, preparing his future, he returned to Pekin, and was able to get back to his usual work, in collaboration with Dr. Black, director of the Geological Service of the Rockefeller Foundation. Once more circumstances favoured him. In a letter of 11 November 1933, he gives the following account of his discoveries:

'Clearing-away operations at Chou-Kou-Tien have led to the discovery of a neighbouring cave, completely full up also, but younger, and containing abundant traces (two human skulls), implements of stone and bone, collars of pierced teeth, varied and extinct fauna of an Upper Palaeolithic culture (the age of the reindeer in France). Lower down, on the other hand, we have the proof that before being inhabited by *Sinanthropus*, the rocks were peopled by baboons. That becomes complicated and curious. I continue to have most of the responsibility for interpreting the facts.'

And this responsibility increased, through the sudden death, in March 1934, of Dr. Black, so that until the nomination of a successor, the whole direction of the excavations fell on Père Teilhard's shoulders. This death started a whole train of conflicting thoughts and feelings. First, there was genuine sorrow. Davidson Black died of heart failure at the height of his powers: 'He had just been talking in a lively way, with his friends,' Teilhard told the abbé Breuil, 'full of plans, as usual. A moment later he was found dead, near this table, in the Lab. which you know so well, between *Sinanthropus* and the *Upper Cave*.' And again: 'A fine death, but it leaves a terrible gap. We shall have to close the ranks to continue the work.'

But alongside these impressions he showed that such a violent disappearance had made him think more deeply: '. . . What an absurd thing life is, on the surface,' he wrote, '. . . So absurd that one is thrown back upon a stubborn and desperate faith in the reality and the survival of the Spirit. Otherwise—I mean, if there is no such thing as Spirit—we should be imbeciles not to go on strike against all human effort.' Here again we find the dilemma we have already posed: *either life is absurd or it is divine*. But for him the choice was already made. He was bruised to the very marrow by some of the attitudes of unbelief which followed Black's death. Let us hear his own reaction, in a letter from Nanking to his friends, the Bégouëns (10 April 1934).

'I can't yet judge how much these events are going to influence my future. But I have an impression that the task in front of me is both a precise and a sacred one, in the direction of "the effort of humanity".' And that task?—'In the disorganization that followed on Black's death, and in the oppressive atmosphere of "agnostic" condolences which surrounded it, I took an oath, on the body of my dead friend, to struggle harder than ever to give hope to man's labour and research.'

This death gave him a most intense and concrete sense of 'the colossal vanity of human effort, unless there is some natural, as well as supernatural future for the Universe in the direction of some kind of immortal consciousness'.

However he waited, as always, for a favourable occasion to keep his oath, and while waiting he pushed on with his work more than ever, by agreeing to join his American friend Barbour, along with the Chinese Wong and two other Chinese geologists, in a wide circular tour towards Nanking and the Yangtse. In May he returned to Chou-Kou-Tien, and then set off again with Barbour on the Yangtse, up which they had to sail as far as Chungking. In any case he did not think he could leave China until Black's successor had been appointed. His trip to Chungking was, in fact, done by motor, as far as Chengtu, and then some four hundred miles farther right up to the borders of Tibet. And he said that he learned much on this journey. Hardly had he got back to Pekin when he set off once more towards Honan for four or five weeks. But none of this deflected him from his religious ideal, which he regarded as of primary importance.

## 'HOW I BELIEVE'

In the course of his scientific work of 1934 the call of God came to him in ways which he could not mistake. We must try to understand what was happening. One must remember the writings of a spiritual nature which he had already composed and which were circulating in cyclostyled copies round the Universities and Seminaries. One of the most remarkable of these was *Le Milieu divin*, of 1926–27. He had had very warm praise for this from Louvain and various other places, notably the Theology Faculty of Lyon. But his desire to get the *imprimatur* had not yet been realized. *Le Milieu divin* was still under consideration in Rome. There was also 'The Spirit of the Earth' (*l'Esprit de la Terre*) of 1931, still unpublished. Many who had read these essays, more or less *sub rosa*, carried away the impression of many fine and lofty ideas, but some were so new, and also so vague, that people wondered what exactly he was getting at and in what direction his readers were being led by so powerful and so original a guide.

Among those who followed closely these original notions, and who were extremely anxious to get from Père Teilhard's pen the testimony of a reliable agreement between science and faith, one of the foremost was Mgr Bruno de Solages, the very acute rector of the Institut Catholique of Toulouse. He is referred to in the following letter of Teilhard's, written on 23 September 1934:

'I've made a sketch of an essay which Mgr B. de S. has been asking from me for some time. I call it *Comment je crois* ('Why and how') [sic]. ... It's a study which makes me analyse my position and boil it down a bit better. I am determined to go through with it and do it as sincerely as I can. ... It is a study of the successive development of a *credo* which, from faith to faith, converges towards and joins up with the Christian current (or *phylum*). Faith in the World, Faith in the Spirit in the World, Faith in the immortality of the Spirit in the World, Faith in the expanding personalization of the World. I fancy I have a better hold now than a year ago on views which enable me to believe in this seriously.'

In another form it is exactly these ideas which we shall find later on when we come to analyse his *Le Phénomène humain* in detail.

He sent this essay to two of his friends, who were enthusiastic about it. At Lyon Père Auguste Valensin (who had a philosopher's mind if ever there was one) called it 'magisterial'. That was what Mgr Bruno de Solages thought too. It was, we remember, exactly what they said at Louvain about his *Milieu divin*. It had, however, to overcome the wise procrastination of Rome. At Rome, in fact, they have to do something like what they do with sea convoys in war-time. In convoys, the swifter vessels have to adapt their speed to that of the slower ones. The Church does not want to prevent eagles from soaring high and looking right into the sun. But she also has to protect the humblest of sparrows and prevent them from being frightened. Père Teilhard knew too that *time* is necessary for the evolution of ideas, and that, as St. Vincent de Paul said, one should not 'run ahead of Providence'. For himself, however, he believed he had always to go right in front. That was his personal mission and he could not betray it. As he wrote at the time, 'One must somehow contrive to keep the zest for life and action, while giving up any idea of happiness for oneself. There lies the secret, and not the illusion, of the "divine milieu".'

About this time too he wrote an essay which he himself said was 'strictly meant for professional friends': 'Christology and Evolution' (*Christologie et Evolution*). It is important to notice this limitation: it shows that he did take account of the fact that his writings were not to be put indiscriminately into everybody's hands and that they might disturb the uninitiate in their faith. In fact he saw he was bound to a certain esoterism, and that is not without importance. In a letter he says confidentially, about this last work, that 'I wrote it from my deepest love of Christ, as an expression of my adoration which I could not keep bottled up inside.' And he adds at once: 'Père Maréchal of Louvain has done me the honour of writing to me about a little paper I sent him, "The place of Man in Nature",[1] which was printed last year in the *Bulletin des étudiants de Pékin*.' Père Maréchal replied: 'Nobody else today holds in his hand, as you do, all the theological, philosophical and scientific data on the problem of evolution.' And Teilhard found this so comforting that he ends at once: 'If this situation is admitted—indeed, if it is true—then it would be to the Church's interest to make use of it.' And a few days later he wrote: 'I still see exactly the same issue in front of me: to go forward further, believing more and more deeply. May the Lord preserve in me a passionate zest for the World, much gentleness, and may He help me to remain fully human to the last.'

[1] Published in *La Vision du Passé* (Oeuvres, vol. III). (Tr.)

## SURVEYS

Along with his spiritual activities, Père Teilhard continued to do his specialist 'surveys' as we have called them. The abbé Breuil came for the second time to Pekin. Teilhard took him to Chou-Kou-Tien and the two scientists discussed together the highly important results of the excavations. They set off together back to Europe, by the Trans-Siberian railway, and when he got to France Père Teilhard was together with his friends in Paris for three months, and was able to give a new impetus to the influence which he exercised over a great number of minds who were attracted to his ideas and had been helped by his spiritual advice.

But on 6th September 1935 he set off again for Bombay. He had been requested from America to take part in a scientific expedition in Kashmir, directed by de Terra. 'They need', he wrote, 'a geologist who knew China—and rightly so. I know the leader personally. I'm not very thrilled at the idea of going to India. But I think it is my strict duty to do my best to go there.'

We shall not follow him through this journey, nor through that which he made afterwards to Java—another survey—in the company of the young and brilliant Koenigswald. All we shall do is to underline the profound evolution during these very years in his heart. Beyond the scientist, beyond the poet or the philosopher, we find, let us call it, the 'prophet' emerging. And that is one of the aspects of his last activities which has been most discussed.

## EVOLUTION

While he was en route for Bombay he pondered, on the steamer, about his final attitude to scientific study. He tried to put his views on 'The Discovery of the Past' (*La Découverte du passé*) in writing, and this was published in *Etudes* in November 1935. From now on he was convinced that it is not the past that matters but the future. Like Polybius he contrasts antiquarian history with the 'pragmatic' history of the statesman. On 8 September 1935, he wrote:

'It's as if, for reasons drawn from the advance of my knowledge itself, the Past and its discovery had ceased to interest me. *The Past has shown me the shape of the Future.*' (Mme Aragonnés' italics.) 'And preoccupation with the future tends to sweep everything else aside. It is essential to establish myself with more firmness than ever as a specialist on the past, precisely in order to speak of the Future with some authority. But it is a curious thing, isn't it, that the object of my work has in some way withered in yielding me its fruit; and that I no longer believe so much in the value of the discoveries I may be able to make, because their interest seems to me henceforth to have been superseded.'

But what is the essential outlook which makes him speak in this way? Here is his reply: 'Now that the fundamental discovery has been made,' he goes on, 'namely that we are borne on by an advancing wave of consciousness, what is there left of importance to discover behind us? Perhaps certain rhythms or springs which are hidden from us by the tenuousness of the present moment. This is the way I want to ponder about it, so as to keep, if possible, an enthusiasm for Geology for my old age. But what a difference there is, all the same, in the object of my ambitions, between this voyage and that of 1923. I like to think that it is a progress.'

On September 14th, still on board the *Cathay* and en route for India, he wrote to his brother in the same vein: 'My enthusiasm has lost its former freshness. But I like to follow my destiny and trust in it. Never have I had so little idea as to where it is leading me.'

So the prophet in him is still hesitant and a bit nonplussed. But Providence is there, and he does 'follow'. In the course of this voyage, as of others, he was struck by the variety of human groups. Because of this variety he strongly criticizes the attitude of putting all nationalities on the same level: he says it is one of the worst mistakes of our modern egalitarianism. 'The more I see of the East,' he wrote to Max and Simone Bégouën, this same September 14th, 'the more I distrust demogogy in internationalism.' And he explains himself soon after, in a letter of 21 January 1936: 'The more I travel abroad, the more I fear that Geneva (which fundamentally I support), many liberal Catholics, and especially my brethren the Missionaries, make a grave mistake, which is contrary to all biology, in admitting the equality of all races. Universalism is not democracy (=egalitarianism).'

His letters to the abbé Breuil and to his friends the Bégouëns are full of picturesque descriptions of the towns and country he passed through: Bombay, where he disembarked on September 20th, 1935; the Punjab, which he traversed in October; and still more, details about his work as geologist and prehistorian. On November 5th he was able to write: 'I think our work will lay the foundations for Hindu Prehistory, which up till now has remained in limbo.' And again, to the abbé Breuil (18 December): 'You will see that the material from our little expedition may provide a fundamental basis for the Prehistory of India.'

But what comes out most often in his writing is the impression of a summons from Providence: 'As I wrote previously to a friend,' he says on November 15th, 1935, 'I believe that Providence has led me once more to a point which is crucial for my science, and just at the psychological moment.' And more clearly still (21 January 1936), after some new surveys, he wrote to his brother Joseph: 'As you roughly know, my voyage, which I was a bit dubious about undertaking, has been very interesting and productive. . . . To sum up, both in India with de Terra and in Java with Koenigswald, I fell plumb on the two most burning sectors of the Prehistoric front: and precisely at the right moment for decisive attacks which I was able to take part in. It has considerably increased my experience and widened my platform. . . .'

We must note this last word. To him, all his science, as we have for a long time been pointing out, was only a preamble, a preparatory study, a 'platform'. And in this same letter to his brother he explains: 'My science, to which I owe so much, seems to me less and less a sufficient life aim in itself. The true interest in my life has for a long time lain in an effort more fully to find God in the world. It's a more tricky subject, but it's the only vocation I can recognize, and nothing will make me deviate from it.'

## A GLIMPSE OF HIS VOCATION

As he was travelling from Hong Kong to Shanghai, from the 15th to 27th January, he had a sudden glimpse of his vocation. Far from complaining about the length of the journey, he planned to use it in 'concentrating once more upon God and gathering the fruits of recent activity'. And then he went on with a passage in which can be found a whole programme to be completed before his death: 'I think that my vocation has never been so naked and clear: to personalize the world in God.' That is the theme which his thought will in future centre upon and which will appear in his essay of 1936, 'Sketch of a Personal Universe' (*Esquisse d'un Univers personnel*) (unpublished). There he examines in succession the significance of the Person, the prolongation of the Person into Supra-Humanity, the consummation of the Person in God, the energy of personalization through Love, the cosmic sense and the human sense, the religion of the Person, realized in Christianity.

He was aware of the boldness of some of his views, but he was convinced that his attitude was 'supremely Christian'. And so he was ripe, as he thought, to write his great synthesis. All he needed for that was the leisure to do it, and that leisure would itself be the providential sign that he was waiting for. This sign shone for him when the Second World War separated him from the world and immobilized him in Pekin. His book *Le Phénomène humain* was written in fact substantially in Pekin from June 1938 to June 1940, with an appendix or 'Postface' dated from Rome, 28 October 1948.

## LOWER CIVILIZATIONS

We have seen how much he distrusted 'egalitarianism'. He had seen too much of the difference in human levels, in the course of his travels. He was sure that different civilizations are the reflection and the result of the religious faith which inspired them; and he was equally sure that the Christian religion alone possessed the secret of human greatness. What seemed to him most deplorable was the tendency in Christian societies to forget what they owe to their Christianity by stopping short either at a narrow scientism, or at a dead ritualism. And what he saw everywhere in the East helped him to understand Christianity. Here for instance is what he says about women in the country now called Pakistan. On October 21st, 1935, he wrote to the abbé Breuil: 'An entirely Muslim population. I wish you could see the women here, so as to measure what our Western civilization has managed to win for their sisters in Europe. Poor things, prematurely wrinkled, swathed up in their veils, always scared. All that has got to be broken down, and it won't be long either.' And later (19 December), 'In fact there are different human groups, biologically and physically, and they can't be "converted" unless one first transforms them on the human plane. I fancy this convergence is possible. So far as I can judge them, the Hindus have disappointed me. Their creative powers, too, are pretty poor. And one has got to go to India to assess how engulfing and lethal a religion can be which concerns itself only with material things and rituals.'

Later, in April 1936 when Japan was infiltrating everywhere into China under his very eyes, he wrote, still in the same vein: 'It is impossible to imagine such a serenely immoral brutality. In their return the Chinese, unable to resist by force, seem to be rallying and forming a *bloc*, fluid but tenacious, which Japan will have great difficulty in either dividing or assimilating. There's quite a chance that they may have the last word.'

Meanwhile, on this eve of the Second World War, he watched the confused events of international politics closely. While the peoples were getting ready for the most bloody struggles, he kept his great dream of human unification. Unfortunately this dream was, I think, enveloped in expressions which are hard for most of us to comprehend. Try, for instance, the following reflections from May–June 1936—of which one part at least (the second) remains very mystifying:

'I'm fed up with all the contemporary agitation that's going on (and many of my friends think as I do): and I'm distressed to see so many men under the pressure of events falling back into a traditional conservatism. It seems to me that the moment has come to make a clean break in the old material. Fascism, communism, democracy, no longer have any meaning,'—obviously, that's what he disdainfully calls 'conservatism'—'I dream of seeing the best of Humanity regrouping itself round a precise mode of thinking, aiming in the three following directions: Universalism, Futurism, Personalism; and joining the political or economic movement which can show itself technically best able to assure these three conditions. Something needs to be said about all this: I feel it, and I know it.'

## A NEW APOLOGETIC?

At this date it seems that Rome counted on him. It was known that he had a new kind of apologetic in hand. This apologetic is once more summed up in these lines of 13 June 1936: 'Now every human action raises the problem of God, and that problem can't be attacked except by the total effort of human research and experience. Not only does God give an eternal value to the effort of man, but His revelation is a response to the totality of human effort.'

This apologetic which was already known to a certain number of his brethren, struck many of them by its cogency, and perhaps by its veil of mystery. A prelate who was Director of missionary work in France, sent him congratulations and posted him a book with a dedication which was so flattering that he did not dare lend the book out until he had cut out these over-enthusiastic lines. But what was more encouraging to him was that at about the same time, the middle of 1936, a highly-placed member of the Apostolic Delegation in Pekin asked him for a report on the conversion of the world, which would be conveyed discreetly, but directly, to the Centre of the Propaganda at Rome. We know nothing of this report, but what we do know is that Père Teilhard tried his hand out in various essays which come from this period: 'Let us Save Humanity' (*Sauvons l'Humanité*), published in *Etudes* of 20 October 1937, under the title 'The Present Crisis' (*La Crise Présente*).

In the interval he had managed to make a brief stay in Paris, early in summer 1937. He was preparing for a voyage to Burma, along with Helmut de Terra, for January 1938. He had to go to France once again, where the Commission for Higher Studies at the Sorbonne had just offered him a post in the Palaeontological Laboratory. In fact three different institutions were after him, the Trocadéro, the Museum, and the Monaco Institute, and he chose the second, that of his master, Boule. From Paris he set off at the end of June 1939 for America, aiming to return to China via the Pacific. In the United States he attended scientific congresses, was everywhere received by warm friends, and finally went on to China. There he was caught by the war. This, he thought, was the time marked out for him to finish his great work, which he had already begun, called *Le Phénomène humain*.

The importance he attached to it is shown in reflections such as this, of 25 July 1939: 'I can see how far my preoccupations have moved, since 1923, away from exoticism and the earth's crust.'

From now on his work of exploration, in spite of later journeys on the African continent, was almost over. This contact, over twenty-two years, with the Earth of Men had wonderfully prepared him for what he considered the supreme aim of his life—about which he had written to his brother Joseph, in a letter from Burma on 13 February 1938: '. . . I am writing for my hour (if it ever comes) and I am patiently working away at my "message" (?) and my platform. It seems to me more important to create a new conception of human activity than to join in the heady fever of a political game which has already got its leaders and will always find its adherents. I follow none the less anxiously the strange changes we are undergoing without much understanding them.'

These lines are a good introduction to the study of *Le Phénomène humain* which will occupy the next chapter. And we can put into the same category the following reflection which he made in Pekin (5 August 1938), while he was working at his book and message: '. . . All the same, I can't help laughing at myself when I see myself so absorbed by the description of a fossilized bone!'

## CHAPTER SIX

# His Message: The Phenomenon of Man (*Le Phénomène humain*)

### AN OUTSTANDING BOOK

AFTER all we have seen of its origins we can hardly think of *Le Phénomène humain* as just one book among others. It is, as we have said, more than a book, it is a 'message'; one might even say it is a sort of 'destiny'. It sums up a whole career, a whole life, and that is the life of a scientist and a priest, a religious dedicated by special vows to the service of Jesus Christ. For years this book was being forged in his burning soul. It may astonish us, and may even deceive us, as any human thing can do. It has been in fact the subject of fierce discussions which we have ourselves witnessed. That is all the more reason why we should read it slowly, quietly, without prejudging it and without taking sides, with a resolve to see in it all the good one can find without ignoring the gaps in it, the inadequacies, perhaps the errors which already different critics have seen in it. Whatever we may think of this or that aspect of Teilhard's thought, it ought not to be possible for us to treat this thought, sincere, moving and tempting as it is, without a deep respect and at least without a spirit of justice and loyalty comparable to that which animates the book itself. And the first sample of this justice is to not ask of its author more than he intended to give, not to condemn the book off-hand for failing to give what we may want to find there but which he has left for us to supply ourselves.

It opens by a 'Warning' of which we should take careful note: 'To be properly understood,' says Père Teilhard, 'the book I am offering here needs to be read not as a work of metaphysics, still less as a sort of theological essay, but only and exclusively as a scientific memoir.' So that is clear. It is a scientist speaking to his peers. He speaks the language they know and love. He treats of the subjects with which they are familiar: matter, atoms, the evolution of life, the animal origins of man, the greatness of the human factor. There is no question of infringing on theological teaching, but of leading the thoughtful scientist to the porch of the temple, of conducting him there by the hand and by means of the certainties which he admits or of the hypotheses which are current in the circles he frequents. It is a question therefore, as Teilhard says in a very packed Prologue which follows the Preface, of *seeing* and *making others see*. See what? That the whole World has a key which can explain it, and that this key is, from the phenomenal point of view, Man. It was already customary to regard man as a *microcosm*, a summary of the Universe. Teilhard, without saying so, takes up this idea. Man is the top-most jewel of Life, and Life has expanded to the very heart of the Universe.

Hence the three divisions of the book: Pre-Life, Life and Thought. We already know Pascal's Three 'Orders'—Matter, Thought and Supernatural Life; and Péguy's Five Realms: the Realm of the Mineral, the Vegetable, the Animal, the Human, and the Christian Realm. Teilhard presents us with a vast continuity in which he distinguishes two main 'thresholds', that of life and that of thought. At the end of his Prologue he salutes the sacred moment when man 'discovers that he is not an element lost among cosmic solitudes, but that there is a universal will to live which converged upon him and "hominized" in him'. And he concludes: '*Man is not a static centre of the World, as has so long been thought: he is the axis and the "arrow" of Evolution, which is something much finer.*' (p. 36.)

## PRE-LIFE

The Pre-living is what we usually call matter. In calling it 'Pre-Life' Teilhard wants to imply already that there is a direction, a tendency, an obscure sort of will in matter: Life.

In matter he distinguishes three things: *Plurality*, by virtue of which 'the substratum of the tangible Universe, dizzily numerous and minute, slopes down towards a limitless base, disintegrating as it goes'. (p. 41.) Next, *Unity*, which pushes the elements towards each other so as to comprehend them together in one great whole, the Universe. And finally *Energy*, or capacity for interaction, which is no doubt 'the most primitive form of the Stuff of the Universe'. And the immediate consequence of this is that the World forms 'a System by its Plurality; a Totum by its Unity; and a Quantum by its Energy'. (p. 43.)

But what is new in our contemporary conceptions of matter is that instead of seeing it, as in the last century, under the twin categories of fixity and geometry, we can now only see it under the twin categories of duration (*la durée*) and of evolution. The whole Universe, in fact, is found to be engaged in an immense evolution, to which astronomy claims to be able to assign an initial date: between five billion five hundred million and eight billion five hundred million years. In the course of this colossal evolution the different elements named in chemistry appeared. Père Teilhard as he goes through the list beginning with Hydrogen, only gets as far as Uranium, with atomic weight of 92. We have known for some time that physicists have extended the list as far as an atomic weight of 101, which they have called *Mendelevium*. But it is considered certain that the heavy elements only appeared by way of evolution, starting from lighter ones, that is starting at the bottom from hydrogen. We can say with assurance, as Père Teilhard does, that 'the stars are laboratories in which, going in the direction of huge molecules, the Evolution of Matter occurs.' (p. 50.)

Teilhard recalls at this point that two principal laws rule matter: that of the conservation of energy and that of the degradation of energy into heat. No doubt he did not know the recent theory of the Cambridge school, whose instigator is Mr. Fred Hoyle, according to which, for the Universe to remain 'stationary', new atoms are incessantly being created, whose total one can calculate in the mass as fifty thousand stars a second! Or if he did know this theory, which anyway is in dispute, he did not take account of it. He paid special attention to the law of the degradation of energy, or entropization, and he writes: 'The more the Quantum of energy in the World functions, the more it gets used up.' Here again like recent astrophysicists, he might have given statistics. The sun, they say, 'burns' four million tons of its hydrogen per second, and they calculate that it will be at the end of its term after the passage of from twelve to fifteen billion years. It is certain then that Time plays an immense rôle in the Universe. Time itself began, gets used up, it ends. Teilhard writes on this: 'A rocket which soars up, following the arrow of Time, and only expands in order to burn out—an eddy which travels up-stream in the middle of a descending current: that must be the figure of the World. That's what Science says. And I believe in Science. But has Science so far taken the trouble to look at the World otherwise than *from the outside* of things?' (p. 52.)

## THE INSIDE OF THINGS

With these last words Teilhard raises a very important problem, which he calls 'the Inside of Things'. There is, in fact, at least with certain things, an 'Inside'. In our case it is consciousness, or the soul. In animals a kind of consciousness certainly exists, whatever Descartes may have thought. Even plants, as Claude Bernard used to say, obey a 'directive idea'. Professor Richet goes to the extreme point of speaking of a 'cellular intelligence'. But that is not enough for Père Teilhard, and here we reach one of the most disputed points of his vast synthesis. According to him one can state the following universal postulate: 'There is an Inside of Things, co-extensive with their Outside.' (p. 56.) Or again: 'In a coherent view of the World, Life inevitably implies a Pre-Life preceding it and disappearing out of sight.'

When we read such an affirmation we rub our eyes, we are startled, and we say: 'But surely he is extrapolating.' The postulate he offers us is unverifiable. The proofs he tries to give of it are themselves only baseless assertions. Here is his principle: 'When carefully observed, even only from one point, a phenomenon necessarily, by virtue of the fundamental unity of the World, has ubiquitous value and roots.' (p. 56.) And again: 'Consciousness, when refracted backwards in Evolution, displays itself qualitatively in a spectrum of varying shades whose lower terms are lost in the night.' (p. 59.) It seems that critics, whether sympathetic or hostile, will agree here to refuse to follow Père Teilhard in his audacious conjecture. His 'extrapolation', under the name of 'panpsychism', will be dumped at his door. It comes neither from science nor from philosophy nor theology, but simply, one might say, from a poetic imagination.

That would matter very little if we did not find straight away that Teilhard makes this construction the very basis of his whole *vision* of the World. In fact he establishes a close relationship between the Outside and the Inside of things, and formulates the following law: 'A consciousness is the more complete the more its counterpart is a richer and better organized material edifice.' And he makes it more precise in the following terms, which he italicizes in his own text: '*Spiritual perfection (or conscious "centredness") and material synthesis (or complexity) are merely the two aspects, or partners, of one and the same phenomenon.*' (p. 60.) And finally he leads up to what he calls the '*great Law of complexity and consciousness*; a law implying *a structure, a converging psychic curvature of the World upon itself*'. (p. 61.) True, he knows and says that the parallelism between Matter and Mind is not exact. 'What different thoughts, for the same piece of bread!' he exclaims. We must not press too far, then, his *Law of convergence*, or of *recurrence*, as he likes to call it. But he thinks he can escape both monism and dualism by saying, (1) that it is certainly true that '*all energy* is of a psychic nature'; but, (2) that this fundamental energy—including that of the atom—is divided into 'two distinct components', a *tangential* energy, which brings the energy into solidarity with all elements of the same order, and a *radial* energy, which draws it in the direction of a state ever more complex and ever more directed towards the future.

## LIFE!

It is armed with these two laws that Teilhard tackles the problem of the appearance of Life. We can only examine this problem on our Earth. No doubt Life exists elsewhere, and Teilhard in one of his writings formally subscribes to the hypothesis (which we find as attractive as he does) of the 'plurality of Worlds', but which can only be a hypothesis. Let us see, then, what has happened in the case of the Earth, since we inhabit it and are beginning to understand its history. Teilhard starts off from an affirmation which will certainly raise theologians' eyebrows, and which seems to us a flagrant contradiction within his own thought. He writes, in fact: 'The Earth was probably born by chance.' 'Certainly not', the theologian will reply: 'The Earth was born by a divine decree.' The word 'chance' cannot be admitted into the vocabulary of a genuine believer nor that of a thinker. Nothing happens by chance. However that may be, Teilhard, following the line of his universal pan-psychism, says that 'from the very fact of the individualization of our planet, a certain mass of elementary consciousness was imprisoned to begin with in terrestrial Matter. . . .' The Earth, like all the rest of the Universe, had in it a certain specific quantity of 'Pre-Life'. (p. 72.) So it is not so surprising that one day, when our Earth had suitably cooled off, a prodigious phenomenon should have occurred which Teilhard describes as follows: 'Ultramicroscopic grains of protein densely covered the surface of the Earth, over a depth of several kilometres, in the water, in the air, in the mud which settled.' (p. 72.) That is what he calls 'a Pre-Biosphere'. And here the poet in him breaks out: 'Leaning and looking over the depths of the Past, watch the colour changing. From one age to another the hues are mounting. Something is going to burst out on the young Earth. Life! Look, Life!'

'What's this?' you will say. 'Is Life then only a new state of Matter?' But you will remember in Père Teilhard's first article the notion of the 'critical threshold', which we then said we should meet again. Here it is. Teilhard then cited the well-known and undeniable fact of the piston which remains motionless up to the pressure of one kilogram, and which suddenly moves when the *critical threshold* of one kilogram is passed. In reality this movement of the piston began virtually from the moment of application of the most moderate pressure. According to Teilhard the same is true with Life. It begins virtually from the formation of the atom, but it does not 'burst out' until the critical threshold is reached. And Teilhard writes, rather daringly: 'We have known for some time that there is no precise limit that can be drawn between the animal and the vegetable at the level of monocellular beings. And less and less can we point to a sure barrier (as we shall recall later) between "living" protoplasm and "dead" proteins at the level of very large cellular masses.' That is categorical enough. It would seem then that Père Teilhard admits, at least at the origin of Life and in unique conditions, what is called *spontaneous generation.* Theologians have nothing to say to that. All the great theologians of the Middle Ages, and many others too in modern times, have admitted spontaneous generation. But what has Science thought of it since Pasteur? It appears that Père Teilhard himself hesitated to pronounce on it, for he writes clearly that '. . . one thing is certain: that such a metamorphosis' (that of 'the living from the pre-living') 'cannot be explained by a simply continuous process. By analogy with everything we are taught from the comparative study of natural developments, we have to postulate, at this particular moment of terrestrial evolution, a maturation, a moulting, a threshold, a crisis of the first magnitude: *the beginning of a new order.*' At last! This 'new order' is that which he calls a bit further on (p. 86) the 'cellular Revolution'. And he describes it thus: 'The essential originality of the Cell seems to me to have been to find a new method of enclosing into a unity a larger mass of Matter.' To which we are tempted to reply that the Cell (even with the capital letter that Teilhard gives it) has not 'found' anything at all, for it is itself that has been found!

Here again, in our view Teilhard has not explained anything: he is 'poetizing'. Listen to the triumphant tones in which he celebrates 'the astonishing spectacle presented by the final blossoming of Life on the surface of the young Earth. This spouting out of spontaneity. This luxuriant unfolding of fantastic creatures. This reckless expansion. This leap into the improbable. . . .' (p. 89.) And he is right to wonder at it. We do too. But this does not take us one step further towards the scientific knowledge of 'why' and 'how'. He himself hesitates between two hypotheses: either this explosion of Life happened only once, or else it is only reproduced at cyclic intervals so spaced out (as happens in astronomy) that the phenomenon escapes our limited experience. At present Matter appears 'dead'. It might however, he thinks, wake up again, in conditions which we cannot foresee. It seems as if it is this second hypothesis which he finds more attractive. (p. 98–9.)

### THE BIOSPHERE

We have nothing very important to summarize from the pages which follow, describing the 'initial appearances of Life' and then 'the expansion of Life', for we are obliged to stick to the main lines of Teilhard's synthesis. Though we may note in passing what he says very justly about the *Profusion*, the *Ingenuity*, and finally the *Indifference* of Life to everything that has been superseded, exhausted, by-passed. And we shall pass rapidly also over (*a*) the aggregates of growth, giving rise to 'phyla'; (*b*) the florescence (or disjunctions) of maturity, which periodically produce 'verticils'; and (*c*) the effects of distance in the past, which prevent the evolutionary 'stems' from being traceable. These are, it would seem, glimpses meant for specialists in palaeontology. The very interesting details of them may be found in Père Teilhard's book itself.

Everything he says, in these weighty pages, concerns what he calls the *Biosphere*, the sphere of Life, which is superimposed upon the Barysphere or the Hylosphere, i.e. the sphere of Matter. And he is right to underline that '*the place occupied by the development of Life in the general history of our Planet*' is not only immense in its extension, but also, still more, in its depth, its richness, in (to sum up) its *value*.

Admittedly that word, *value*, which is anthropomorphic, was not actually his word. But he is evidently thinking of it all the time. Life ascends. It does not remain at the same level. It is a continual growth, with 'fumblings' which must not be confused with just 'hazard' but with 'directed hazard'. (p. 110.)

This means that Life, in spite of the apparent fanciful luxury of its forms, *has a direction*, and that this direction can be seen particularly in the appearance of a *nervous system* and in the advance *towards the greatest cerebralization*. That is how the passage from the *Biosphere* to the *Noosphere* can be explained: above Life there is Thought.

### THOUGHT

Here we must give the actual text:

'At the end of the Tertiary era the psychic temperature in the cellular world had been rising for more than five hundred million years. From Branch to Branch, from Layer to Layer, the nervous systems, as we have seen, had advanced and at the same time had become more complex and more concentrated. Finally with the Primates an instrument was constructed which was so supple and so rich that the immediately next step was bound to lead to the whole of animal psychic nature being remodelled and consolidated upon itself. But the movement did not stop there: for nothing in the structure of the organism prevented it from advancing. At the Anthropoid stage, carried up 'mentally' to boiling point, a few extra calories were added. With the Anthropoids, having reached practically the tip of the cone, a last effort was made following the same axis. And no more was needed for the whole inner equilibrium to be reversed. (p. 168.) What was it that happened, then? For ourselves, we should put it thus: In an organism which had reached the point of evolution that He willed, God created a human, an intelligent, and a free soul. In a note to p. 169 Teilhard formally authorizes us to speak in this way. But since he wanted, as he says, to limit himself to the Phenomenal, that is to say to 'empirical relations between Consciousness and Complexity, without prejudice to the action of deeper causes, controlling the whole operation', he does not go further than to say that the 'tangential' energy which had been at work from the very start of the Universe, led, through the 'tiniest little growth' from the Anthropoid to Man, to a turning back of 'radial' energy. And this turning back, this falling back of energy upon itself because it had reached the term of its growth, is what we call *reflection*—a turning back, if ever there was one. But reflection is nothing other than Thought. If you call consciousness C, then thought must be called $C^2$. Animals possess C; only man is characterized by $C^2$. And reflection enables man to say 'I'. This is a veritable revolution. And so appears, at the heart of the created Universe, *the Person*. (All the same, one wonders here how far the appearance of reflection and of personalization is illuminated by Teilhard's theory of tangential and radial energy.)

One thing is sure, both to us and to Père Teilhard: that man is at the summit of the new creation. Our biblical texts are full of this fact. With the appearance of Man it is the whole of nature which has made a 'step' forward. The Hylosphere is at the basis of all. The Biosphere however surrounds it everywhere. And now appears the No-osphere which after humble beginnings (there is always that stem which is hidden from us) has ended, under our very eyes, by dominating the entire Globe.

## THE GREATNESS OF MAN

Père Teilhard has some fine passages on the unique greatness of man in the series of beings. In one of his last writings, dated from New York (25 March 1954), he has this phrase which recalls what we have just said about C and $C^2$. 'With "consciousness squared"', he said, 'we have nothing less than a new species of Life—it is a Life to the 2nd degree—starting its particular evolution during Pliocene times on our planet.' And a bit further on, 'As a consequence, in Man it is not just one phylum more which is branching off at the top of the Primates. It is the world itself which, by forcing its way into a domain that up till then had remainèd closed, starts off again towards itself on a new stage of the way.'

We must understand this fully so as to get to the bottom of his ideas. He was certainly right to protest against the habit there is in zoology of classifying Man purely and simply in a genus, in the vast company of the Vertebrates. In this book *Le Phénomène humain*, he had already well said: 'Here the disproportion hits the eye, which falsifies every classification of the living world (and, indirectly, every construction of the physical world too), in which Man figures only logically as a genus or a new family. That is an error of outlook which distorts and debases the whole phenomenon of the universe. To give Man his real place it is not enough to open a supplementary section within the framework of systematic classification—not even to call him one Order or one Branch more. . . . By hominization, in spite of the insignificance of the economic jump, a new Age begins. The Earth grows a "new skin". Better still, it discovers its soul.' (p. 182.)

'Man came in without any noise,' he says again. But—and this, as we have already pointed out, was always one of his essential ideas—it is not by the lowliness of its origins that we should judge the importance of a phenomenon, but rather by the extent of the developments it engenders. It is not by the weightiness of *Sinanthropus*, or the coarseness of form of Neanderthal man, nor even by the marvellous art with which the Cro-Magnon decorated the walls of the caves he lived in thirty thousand years ago, that we must judge of the greatness of Man, but rather by the scientific discoveries and ultra-modern techniques, on the one hand, and also the purity, the beauty and the holiness of Him who willed to be called 'the Son of Man', and of all the saints who have imitated Him and will imitate Him till the end of the world.

We must judge always by the acorn and the oak. Man is great not merely because he has already covered a great number of stages and experienced a great many turning-points in his history, but also because of all the stages and turnings which he is ready to broach in the future.

And what do we see in our day? Père Teilhard tells us in these highly descriptive lines: 'The earth smoking with factories, pulsating with commerce, vibrating with hundreds of noval radiations. This great organism lives in fact only for, and because of, a new spirit in it. Beneath the changes of the age there is a change in Thought. But where are we to look for or situate this subtle and revolutionary change which without appreciably altering our bodies has made new beings of us?—where but in a new intuition, which modifies from top to bottom the physiognomy of the Universe in which we move: in other words, in an awakening.' (p. 215.)

## OUR NEW DIMENSIONS

For everything has changed in our conception of the universe during the past century. Space and Time have taken on a meaning for us which up till then was unknown. The conquest of Space was the first to take place. Our terrestrial globe, formerly the centre of the World, has shrunk before our eyes. 'The Earth, a mere grain of sidereal dust,' as Teilhard says. And already his data on modern astronomy are out of date, so quickly are new discoveries made in this realm. Our sun has become just one of the stars among the hundred billion which form our galaxy, and this galaxy itself is just one among the billions of others also peopled with stars and no doubt with thinking beings like ourselves, and all these are scattered over the spaces explored by our giant telescopes.

And Time too has lengthened. We have been able to date our Universe, our Sun and our Earth. And this takes us a long way beyond the 4004 B.C. which our forebears admitted. As for Man himself, Prehistory has pushed back his origins to hundreds of thousands of years, and this has modified all our former perspectives. The scientists know this already: tomorrow schoolchildren will be made to learn it and recite it in their lessons.

## AND EVOLUTION

But in Père Teilhard's eyes the most serious revolution which has happened in our knowledge of the world and of ourselves is the replacement of fixity by evolution.

No doubt it was known that everything moves, everything changes. Heraclitus said many centuries ago that 'all flows' and that 'you cannot step twice into the same river'. Nearer our time the famous poet wrote:

Aimez ce que jamais on ne verra deux fois.[1]

But the idea of what Teilhard calls 'irreversible coherence' only came into all the different sciences recently. We are beginning to believe that the very laws of nature are in constant evolution. Paul Dirac, a physicist of the front rank, born in 1902 and a professor at Cambridge, voiced the hypothesis not long ago that the 'fossilized light' which comes to us from galaxies situated a thousand million light-years away is not the same as ours! So for Teilhard evolution is in inescapable evidence.

'For many people', he says, 'Evolution is still only Transformism; and Transformism itself is only an old Darwinian hypothesis, as local and decrepit as Laplace's conception of the solar system, or Wegener's theory of Continental Drift. But it is blindness not to see the extent of a movement whose orbit goes far outside the natural Sciences, and which has successively conquered and invaded from all sides Chemistry, Physics, Sociology, and even Mathematics and the history of Religions. One after the other all the domains of human knowledge are being shattered and then pulled together, by one single undercurrent, towards the study of some sort of development.

'Is Evolution a theory, a system, a hypothesis? . . . No: but much more. It is a general condition to which all theories, all hypotheses and all systems must conform, if they are to be true or even thinkable. Evolution is a light which clarifies all facts, a curve which all features must follow.' (p. 219.) It would be difficult to be more downright and categorical than that!

[1] Love that which you will never see twice—Alfred de Vigny [1797–1863].

## CHAPTER SEVEN

# The Prophet

### TOWARDS THE FUTURE

WE are starting a new chapter, not because we have finished our analysis of Teilhard's book but because at this point there is a change in his own exposition. We know already from the lessons of all his life that in his view science has as its principal task to clarify man's route. It was not the study of fossils which excited him but what those fossils could tell us of our present and of what is waiting for us in the immediate and distant future. In him the scientist was a preparation for the prophet. We have heard him many times over talking about his 'platform'. In his book he gave two hundred and forty pages to constructing that platform. The last hundred he used to express what he called his 'message'. The past is full of lessons for him and for us. That is because the law of evolution, which he has seen at work all along the history of matter and of life, shows itself to him in similar forms in the present: and he uses it to 'extrapolate'—his own word, this time—by extending the trajectory into the future. In his view this trajectory is a long series of inventions and discoveries. There is no reason why it should stop. The very processes of this advance into the future are remarkably similar. The law of the Evolution of things is the only law which itself does not evolve. Thus:

'The instinctive gropings of the first cell join up, on the same trajectory, with the gropings of scientists in our laboratories. . . . The wave which we feel pass through us did not start in us. It comes to us from far away—it set off at the same time as the light from the first stars. It comes to us after having created everything on the way. *The spirit of research and conquest is the permanent soul of evolution.*' (p. 224.) The italics of the last sentence are ours: it contains the whole prophetic message of Père Teilhard.

## MAN'S MISSION

If man is no more, as he so long believed, the centre of the Universe, he is 'something much finer', the 'soaring arrow' of the great biological synthesis. He is this arrow become *conscious*. Man knows from now on that he 'holds in his hands the future of the Universe'.

'Greatness or slavery?' asks Teilhard. The answer is both: together. And this is what partly explains 'the age of anxiety'. This anxiety is stressed by all observers. St. Augustine spoke of it long ago in a famous phrase of his *Confessions*. To him this anxiety was *the need for God*. By novel routes Teilhard reaches the same conclusion. And he spends some time analysing the reasons for our contemporary anxiety. He sees it first as 'Space-Sickness', that is to say, the anguish of man who knows himself lost in the immense sidereal spaces. But it is also 'Number-Sickness', the dizzying thought of all that has been, all that is and will be: the sickness of sheer multitude, and of the unknown open before us. And there is 'Impasse-Sickness', says Teilhard, 'the anguish of feeling oneself shut in', and also of feeling oneself caught in the wheels of Evolution without knowing where it is leading.

## 'NOUS SOMMES EMBARQUÉS'[1]

But whatever our anxiety, we have to go forward. The great game is on, and 'we are the players, and at the same time the cards and the stakes'. (p. 230.) The greatest danger we run is that of asking: 'Is the game worth-while? Or are we being duped?' Père Teilhard can hear, as we all can, the murmurs of disgruntlement, expressions of 'la nausée'[2] and of defiance. If these murmurs should prove true, the situation would be grave. Man would be shrugging off his task, deserting his mission. Speaking of the organized 'strikes' of the last century, Père Teilhard says, 'The next century will certainly not end without seeing the threat of a strike in the No-osphere.'

So far, however, there is nothing to fear. Research is hard at it. The philosophy of 'la nausée' itself ends up paradoxically in a morality of 'engagement'. The world is absurd all right, but let us go forward all the same! Teilhard does not think, however, that this will be sufficient to survive long. He writes: 'Even with the heaps of material energy,

[1] Pascal: 'We are embarked.' [2] 'nausea'—Sartre.

even with the spur of fear or direct desire, Humanity would, without the will to live, soon cease to invent and to create for a work which it knew was condemned in advance. And if it was infected by nausea or revolt at the very source of the life which sustains it, it would disintegrate and tumble into dust.' (p. 232.) And on the following page he formulates the dilemma which he has envisaged all his life:

'Either Nature is closed to our need for a future: and then Thought, the fruit of millions of years of effort, will be still-born and stifled in an absurd Universe, will be a self-induced abortion.

'Or else an open way out does exist: a super-soul above our souls. But in that case, if we are to agree to commit ourselves to it, this issue must open without restrictions upon psychic spaces to which there must be no limit, in a Universe to which we can recklessly entrust ourselves.'

We have to choose then between 'optimism or absolute pessimism'. His choice is already made. Why? Because the past takes responsibility for the future. 'The World is much too big an affair. Right from the earliest beginnings it has, in order to beget us, played miraculously with too many improbables for there to be any risk in our committing ourselves further, right to the end, in its train. If it has undertaken the work that is because it can accomplish it by following the same methods and with the same infallibility with which it started off.' (p. 234.) Reading that, we add in a whisper what the ancients used to say: *Natura non deficit in necessariis!*[1]

## SURVIVAL

And this leads Père Teilhard in his fourth part to treat of Survival, that is, of the immortality of the soul.

But he will not consider this as an individual problem. No one has the right to isolate himself or to claim the existence of an elect race. The circular shape of the Earth has had the result, according to Teilhard, of throwing us upon each other. This is now more true than ever. The human density on the earth has not ceased to increase. Humanity forms a whole in which all have need of all. Biologically men are brothers: for there is this between them—'Indefinite inter-fecundation, at every level. Blending of genes. Anastomes of races in civilizations and political bodies.' (p. 241.) Humanity is not merely cosmopolitan: alone among living beings it is literally *planetary*. So the future is preparing for us, beyond the two opposing *blocs* of today, a muster of all men into one

[1] Nature does not fail in necessities.

single *bloc*. From now on from the economic point of view 'it is the whole Earth that is needed to feed each one of us'. (p. 246.)

It is obvious that henceforth scientific Research must be international: it has become 'something like a common activity of knowledge and performance'. But what is the direction of science? Not only towards knowledge, but 'also and perhaps still more towards *knowledge for the sake of ability*'. And that means, of course, '*greater ability for the sake of greater activity*. But finally, and above all, *greater activity for the sake of BEING more*.'

## HIS GREAT DREAM

In his enthusiasm as prophet and precursor Père Teilhard does not hesitate to make the most extraordinary extrapolations. Speaking of the perhaps imminent possibility of manufacturing Life in the laboratory, he writes:

'Yes, the dream which human Research unconsciously draws upon is, basically, that of being able to control, beyond all atomic or molecular affinities, the fundamental Energy which all other energies merely subserve: having brought all its elements together, to be able to direct the World, by putting its finger upon the very spring of Evolution.' (p. 250.) And he adds, weighing his words, 'To those who have the courage to admit that their hopes do indeed travel as far as this, I would say that they are the most human of humans today—and that there is less difference than one might think between Research and Adoration.'

But he recognizes that to reach that point it will be necessary to get past many contemporary hesitations, oppositions and separations. This will be a new *critical threshold* to face. 'Modern man no longer knows what to do with the time and the powers which he has unleashed and now holds in his hands.' This means that 'a new domain of psychic expansion' must open up before us. Of what sort will it be? Teilhard sees it in the form of 'an inner "totalization" of the World upon itself —the unanimous construction of a *Spirit of the Earth*'. (p. 253.)

## IS THIS POSSIBLE?

We may wonder whether these predictions are acceptable, whether this dream is not a mad one, whether indeed there is not a risk here of putting ourselves in the place of God Himself. Teilhard repudiates the hopes based on the 'Future of Science' of people like Renan, Berthelot and many others; but he is sure that science has not had its last word. He writes—still 'extrapolating'—'In the direction of Thought, as in the direction of Time and Space, can the Universe terminate anywhere else than in the Measureless?' (p. 252.) To those who are discouraged or impatient, he points to the past: 'Why! half-a-million, perhaps a million years were needed for Life to pass from the Prehominids to modern Man; and now, just because less than two centuries after having sighted a still higher state above him, this modern Man is still in the throes of struggling to disentangle himself from himself, we already begin to despair! . . . Each dimension has its own rhythm. So, for a planetary movement we need a planetary kind of poise. . . . We must calm our impatience and take courage.' (p. 255.)

Obviously at this moment we are floundering around, groping. Indeed perhaps at this moment there is even *regression*? That has happened in history. And how are we to know whether we are going in the right direction? Well, consider the results. 'The great human machine is made to advance—and it must advance—by producing a superabundance of Mind. If it is not working, or rather if it engenders nothing but Matter—then that must be because it has gone into reverse. . . .' (p. 257.)

But that is what seems to be happening. In our 'mass movements' we are travelling towards the *Impersonal*, towards the 'ant-heap'. Yet the whole course of Evolution seems to suggest precisely the opposite: it urges us forward towards more consciousness, more personality, more brotherly union.

'Evolution . . . is an ascent towards Consciousness. . . . It is only towards a hyper-reflection, that is, towards a hyper-personalization, that Thought can extrapolate itself.' (pp. 258 f.) We are the consciousness of the Universe. But to have a meaning, this consciousness must be *centred*. In fact it is so, for it converges towards a point which will blend together and bring all the 'layers' of evolution to their consummation. This point is the mysterious, but necessary, one which Teilhard calls '*the Omega point*'. As he says in a letter we have quoted earlier, beyond the Universe we have to 'seek the OTHER'.

## NO PANTHEISM

How can this 'Omega point' be of any interest to us? Uniquely because in it we find our full development, the way in which we can go to the uttermost of ourselves, by remembering precisely that we have no end in ourselves but that at our deepest levels there is in us a thirst for the infinite. And it is here that, as we have already said, Père Teilhard by a new route reaches the same point as St. Augustine of Hippo.

Marxism, he notes, believes that to respond to this profound need of our nature it is enough that each of us should bequeath his works, his discoveries, his artistic creations, or simply the fruit of his efforts, to humanity. But this is to miss the fact that our principal work is not in what we do but in what we become in our inmost personality. Man is the final crown of nature. So the 'Omega point' should act as a rallying-point for all human persons. 'Our "I",' writes Teilhard, 'our personality precisely. Deeper than all its radiations, the very centre of our consciousness—this is the essential thing that the Omega must retrieve in order genuinely to be an Omega.' And at this point Teilhard condemns all kinds of pantheism because they bury the individual in the great Whole. '*Union differentiates*', he says, and rightly underlines it. One only unites what subsists: when things are destroyed, union ceases. The real problem then is that of Union, which welds individuals together without annihilating them. 'And', concludes Teilhard, 'that exactly brings us to the problem of love.'

## LOVE-ENERGY

Obviously this does not refer to any kind of love, nor to a love which can be chiefly defined by the feelings it arouses. Considered in its full biological reality, love (that is, the affinity of one being to another) is not confined to Man. It represents a general property of Life. But in Man it takes on an exceptional importance. 'Under the compelling power of love it is fragments of the World which seek after each other so that the World may come into being.' (p. 265.) Love is the source of the Union which welds individuals together without destroying their precious personality but fulfilling it. 'Love alone takes and joins together human beings at the deepest part of themselves; and for that reason love alone—this is a fact of everyday experience—is capable of fulfilling human beings, *quâ* human beings, by reuniting them.' (p. 265.) Henceforward Love is the necessary and sufficient agent by which Humanity, the Spirit of the Earth, the Synthesis of individuals and of peoples, the paradoxical reconciliation of the Part and the Whole, of the One and the Many (all of which seem *à priori* to be utopian notions, but which nevertheless are biologically necessary) are able to take shape in the world.

Once this point has been well established it will help us to understand the reality of the 'Omega point' towards which human energies are moving whether they know it or not. Since love alone can 'unite', the point of convergence of all human loves must be, at the summit of the World above our heads, 'something Loving and Lovable'.

Man seems to find it repugnant to bow before a personal God. Our time likes to look below itself and not above. As Père Teilhard says at this point, 'Physics and Biology always look in the direction of some infinitely diluted Matter in order to discover the Eternal and the mighty Stability.' (p. 268.) This is a fundamental mistake which the primitive human ages never made. 'Common sense is right', he says: 'it is impossible to dedicate oneself to some Anonymous Number.' (p. 257.) And he adds: 'The discoveries made in the last century have, by their unitary viewpoint, brought a new and decisive impetus to our conception of the World and of the Earth. Hence the way modern pantheisms have sprung up. But this impetus will only end by plunging us back into some super-materialism, unless it leads us to a person.'

The logic of our need for unity and love suggests to us, then, according to Teilhard, the 'attributes of the Omega point', that is to say of a hidden God towards whom we are advancing and in whom we shall find our completion. It reveals itself already in the laws of our evolution. Nothing can reach completion without love: but 'love dies at the touch of the Impersonal and the Anonymous'. Moreover, 'to love it is essential to coexist'. The Omega point is living. It cannot be a simple 'ideal', a 'virtual centre', because 'a No-osphere which is actual and real must have a Centre which is real and actual. In order to be supremely magnetic, the Omega must already be supremely present.' (p. 269.) And it must also be man's 'reason for survival. We protest against death, which we conceive of as a fall into nothingness. Faith in God is the only one to guarantee us immortality.' The radical defect of all forms of Faith in Progress, such as they are expressed in positivist creeds, is, says Teilhard, 'that they do not completely eliminate Death. What is the use of being able to discern some kind of nucleus at the pinnacle of Evolution if this nucleus must itself one day disintegrate?' That is just what the philosopher Höffding meant when he declared that man's faith in God comes from the need to put all his essential values out of harm's reach. But precisely because Omega is 'the last term in the series, it is at the same time *outside all series* itself. Not only does it crown it: it closes it. . . . If by nature it did not escape the Time and Space which it gathers together, it would not be Omega.' (pp. 270 f.) In these passages and in the whole of his account Teilhard drives away the least suspicion of pantheism. For him, God is eternal. He is not caught in universal Evolution. 'The mighty Stability is not below, in the infra-elementary, but above, in the ultra-synthetic.' That is why Teilhard writes: 'The four attributes of the Omega are: autonomy, actuality, irreversibility, and so, finally, transcendence.'

Even if our material World is subject to entropy, that is, destined to an unavoidable End, which our astrophysicists even try to calculate, we can say that not everything is subject to entropy. Even if we can picture as inevitable 'the fantastic and ineluctable event which draws nearer every day—the end of all life on our globe, the death of the Planet itself, the last phase of the Human Phenomenon'—that does not mean that we believe in the end of everything.

## THE END OF THE WORLD

Teilhard would not be the prophet we have seen him to be if he did not broach the grave problem of the end of the World—a problem which more and more haunts our conversation since the discovery of the atom bomb. He does not actually speak of this bomb, which had not yet exploded at Hiroshima when he was writing his book; but he did want to express his views on the *novissima* of our Universe. He does so, however, 'coldly, logically, without anything apocalyptic: and not so much in order to say anything as to make people think'. (p. 274.)

Accordingly to him, firstly, the end of the World will not come through any sudden catastrophe or sidereal cataclysm. Neither, secondly, will it come 'by slow death in our prison'. In any case astronomers can guarantee us 'several hundred million years', so we can 'breathe again'. Nor finally does Teilhard believe in the predictions of people like Benson, Wells and others, that is, the end of the world coming through Wars, Revolutions, microbe-Invasions, etc. These he considers are the causes of 'individual ends' not of a collective End. Perhaps he would not have spoken with such assurance 'after the Bomb'. He has an incurable optimism. He believes man to be 'irreplaceable'. And man has not finished his task: so the reason for hope lies in what he still has to do. Teilhard reckons he has three major tasks: (i) The organization of Research; (ii) the concentration of this research upon the human object; and (iii) the joining up of Science and Religion. On these three topics he has many rewarding passages, even if we may not have the same robust confidence he has in men's wisdom.

First, he would like to see Research taking a quite new direction. Up till now it has remained grossly utilitarian and materialistic: 'Everything done for production, for armaments. Almost nothing yet for the scientists and the laboratories which multiply our potentialities tenfold.' (p. 279.) Again, 'Less is spent on the annual budget of world research than is spent on one battleship! Our great-grandchildren won't be wrong in thinking of us as barbarians.'

Secondly, what is most backward in Research is 'the human object'. There is so much progress that needs to be made in the training of man, improving his conditions, enlarging his scope of activities, indeed, in the whole *moral realm*. Teilhard here in his own way—which is never the conventional one—touches on the crucial problem.

Nothing is more common among social observers than to deplore the glaring discrepancy between the progress of Science and of Matter, and the moral regress of human beings. We have not got enough laboratories, engineers or atomic centres for the peaceful utilization of the atom. But we are far more cruelly short of moral educators, of those who can reliably guide us towards a purer type of humanity, a finer, a more generous, a less animal, less carnal or earthy humanity. Teilhard reckons that in this field there is vast progress to be made in the future: 'From this point of view we can predict that if we are moving towards a human era of Science, this era will be pre-eminently one of Human Science: when Man who knows will at last see that Man as "object of knowledge" is the key to the whole Science of Nature.' And he outlines a sort of programme: 'First care for, and full development of, the human body: the vigour and health of the organism.' That is because the impetus of the Spirit can only work effectively upon a healthy material base. Then 'the eugenics of individuals—and, as a result, the eugenics of society'. We have to realize a *Human Energetics*.

And that is when Science 'because it has been led to concentrate on man, will find itself more and more face to face with Religion'.

Teilhard condemns the error of the last two generations which have seen the conflict between Science and Faith grow stronger and sharper. He does not blame Renan for his Religion of Science, but he does blame him for believing that Science could replace the spiritual forces which have acted throughout the long past of humanity. Science has its unsurmountable limits: it has need of Faith to pursue its own possibilities to the utmost. 'Neither in its first impetus, nor in its constructions can Science go to its own limits without taking on the tones of mysticism and putting on Faith.' Man in fact cannot go on working unless he has a passionate desire for work. 'But this desire is entirely dependent on the conviction, which Science can't demonstrate, that the Universe has a meaning, and that it can, indeed must, lead, if only we are faithful, to an irreversible Perfection. Hence, a Faith in Progress.' (p. 284.)

In fine, we are dealing with two complementary spiritual forces. 'Religion and Science', says Teilhard, 'are the twin faces of one and the same complete act of knowledge—the only one which can take in the Past and the Future of Evolution in such a way as to study them, measure them and complete them.' (p. 284.)

Further on however he hesitates between two possibilities in the future: either 'ultimate convergence working in tranquillity', or 'Evil growing at the same time as the Good' and reaching its paroxysm at last: this, too, under some specifically novel form. In other words, either 'acceptance or refusal of Omega'.

Teilhard admits that this second hypothesis is 'more like . . . traditional apocalypse'. In that case there would be three evolutionary curves in the future: on one side, the curve of Entropy descending towards the sterility of the planet; on the other side, the ascending curve of Faith and Love; and finally the descending curve of Rejection and Revolt. Teilhard sums up these three curves in the following passage:

'The material exhaustion of the planet, leading to its death; the Noosphere split in two over the form that its unity should take; and, finally, what will show the real meaning and importance of this event, the freeing of that portion of the Universe which has, all through Time, Space, and Evil, refused the laborious task of synthesis to the end.'

When he has finished this part of his exposition, Teilhard is perhaps rightly worried whether many people will not shut the book, 'perplexed and dissatisfied', as he says, 'and wondering whether I have been taking them on a conducted tour through facts, or through metaphysics or dreams'. Those who have followed our analysis thus far may perhaps agree.

## THE CHRISTIAN PHENOMENON

We have constantly said that Teilhard was addressing chiefly modern Man, and more especially those he mixed with all his life, the scientists, seekers, specialists in Palaeontology and Prehistory. And we have also remarked that he only wanted to lead them to the porch of the Temple. So we must not ask of him something which he did not intend to do. However, he could not resist, at the end of his 'message', introducing what he calls *Le Phénomène chrétien*, in an appendix which he calls 'Epilogue'.

In exactly nine pages he tries to show that there is an internal harmony between the biological demands of universal Evolution, such as he has outlined them, and Christianity. He has already postulated an 'Omega point' which is already existing, is alive, and is present in our midst. And of course, the whole of Christianity is based on this certainty, that God is, that He lives, acts, has spoken to men, has willed to guide us in our actions throughout the ages. The Christian phenomenon is a fact which Science cannot ignore. However, Teilhard only wants to look at it from the point of view which he has adopted all through his book:

'Living as I do at the heart of Christianity, I might be suspected of wanting artificially to introduce an apologetic. But here again, and in so far as it is possible for a man to separate different levels of knowledge within himself, it is the naturalist now speaking and asking for a hearing.' (p. 292.)

Christianity is found to answer, point by point, to all the demands of the evolutionary march of Man. What in fact does it teach us? A personal God, a God who is Providence, a God who is Revealer. And this 'leaves a place for, and easily links up with, everything fine and healthy in the Universal'. It is a great mistake to reduce Christianity 'to a soft kind of philanthropy'. 'You fail to understand its mysteries,' says Teilhard stoutly, 'if you don't see it as the most realistic and the most cosmic of all men's faiths and hopes.' Christ came to direct the ascent of humanity. 'Christ is the principle of universal vitality; and because He arose as a man among men, He was in a position to turn, and has been for ever in process of turning in upon Himself the general ascent of the consciousness of men among whom He was born, and so of purifying, directing and vivifying it.' (p. 294.) It is in Him and through Him that 'the total psychic content of the Earth' will be completed. It is through Him alone that the ideal, glimpsed and defined by St. Paul, will be realized—'God will be, and will be all in all.'

Above all Christianity has the merit of existing, of having shown its mettle, of having nourished the highest civilization on earth, and of not having been replaced by any metaphysic, whether Plato's, Spinoza's or Hegel's.

But its deepest element is the power of love which it contains and which it has been spreading for centuries: 'Christian love', says Teilhard, 'is something incomprehensible to those who haven't experienced it. . . . Isn't it a positive fact that for twenty centuries thousands of mystics have drawn from its fire such passionate ardour as to outstrip, in brilliance and clarity, the enthusiasms and devotions of any human love?...' (p. 295.) Make no mistake, it is always this love which gives life to Christianity. If that should die out, 'the enormous structure of rites or hierarchy which the Church represents would fall instantaneously into the dust from which it sprang!'

On the other hand, Christianity remains the sole 'open' religion. No present or future discoveries can surprise or scandalize it. 'For practically all ancient religions, the refashioning of cosmic views characteristic of "the modern mind" have been a crisis from which, if they aren't already dead, one can predict that they won't recover.' Christianity alone can grow up along with Science, expand with it, right to the last limits of Space, measured in billions of light-years.

'In order to live and to develop, Christian views need an atmosphere of expansion and of community.' In fine, 'if the World is convergent, and if Christ occupies its centre, then the "Christo-genesis" of St. Paul and St. John is nothing other, and nothing less, than the expected, yet unhoped-for, prolongation of the No-ogenesis in which, so far as our experience goes, Cosmo-genesis culminates'. (p. 297.)

To summarize: Christianity goes in the same direction as that arrow of Evolution which we have seen flying towards the Omega point. It is, in fact, towards this point, and this alone, that the Christian faith directs us with every impulse of our love.

But we must not get it wrong: it would be false to think and say that Christianity lies in 'the line of nature'. Teilhard knows that well. He knows that we are called to something much higher than nature indicates. And that is why he adds (at the bottom of p. 298) an indispensable footnote. He has just spoken of the Omega point, situated at the summit of the World; and he writes: 'Or rather, a more precise formula, "to confirm the presence, at the summit of the World, of something *in the same line but higher still*, the Omega point".' This is done out of respect for the theological thesis of the 'Supernatural', according to which the unitive contact formed *hic et nunc* between God and the World reaches a supra-intimacy and a supra-gratuity which Man could never have thought of or laid claim to by virtue merely of the demands of his 'nature'.

In concluding Teilhard tries to dispel certain mists in the way of the understanding of his work. And he replies to the three following questions, which no doubt were put to him by more than one interlocutor in the preparation of his book: '(*a*) What place is left to free-will (and so to a possible check to the World's advance)? (*b*) What value is given to the Mind (in relation to Matter)? And (*c*) what distinction remains between God and the World, in the theory of the cosmic Entanglement?'

On the first point he admits that the fact of freedom prevents us from considering the success of Cosmo-genesis as completely determined and assured. He only wanted to trace the main lines, indicate the possibilities and open the way. It remains that to the Christian Providence leads the World to its Destiny even through freedoms which are sometimes, even often, rebellious.

Second, Mind and Matter are like two linked variables; but each of these variables has its laws which neither one nor the other can eliminate or get rid of on to its neighbour.

Third, Teilhard means once for all to have done with 'pantheism'. To do that, he only has to recall what he has said so many times about the *Union which differentiates* without destroying what it unites. God all in all is not the same thing as God absorbing all minds. Quite the contrary, and the point does not need to be laboured.

CHAPTER EIGHT

# The Critics

## A MUCH-DISCUSSED BOOK

SUCH then is this book, whose publication was such an event and which from the moment it appeared gave rise to so much discussion, for and against.

The hardest thing to do when you have finished reading it is to classify it exactly. It gives itself out 'as a scientific memoir'. (p. 21.) But obviously it is something different from, and more than, that. The author may well disclaim writing metaphysics, but it is clear that he very soon goes beyond the mere data of observation. In his last part, especially, the part we analysed under the heading of 'the Prophet', he is no longer doing pure science. He himself, as we have seen, says that the critic may believe he has led him 'into metaphysics or a dream'.

What one must recognize however, before coming to the more or less fierce criticisms of the book, is that we have here an essay of unusual power, of extraordinary originality and of a profundity which is in places unrivalled. Teilhard is far from having solved all the problems, but he has the merit of having presented them to their fullest extent, and of suggesting the necessity, and even the relative ease, of a fundamental agreement between science and faith.

The very success of the book seems to point to its great opportunity. Although it is as a whole difficult to read, by reason of the subject dealt with, of the technical vocabulary, and of the numerous neologisms created by the author, one might say that it has been the object of a sort of plebiscite. The 50,000 copies already[1] distributed—and these no doubt do not exhaust its possible sales—are a good proof of the interest it has aroused. That is why we are not among those who regret its publication. The book will be for everyone an occasion for reflection, for meditation, for restatement, for saying where one stands, and this

[1] Figures for 1957; since then the figure has risen to 70,000 in France alone.

can only contribute to the advancement of the very serious questions which it tackles.

If Teilhard chiefly wanted to throw light on our future, then there may be a hope that our advance towards this future which is still hidden from our eyes may be slightly, however slightly, illuminated and certainly encouraged. His robust optimism has something bracing, and, let us hope, something contagious about it. And he does not hide the fact that this optimism comes to him exclusively from his faith. True, he did not want to write an apologetic. And it is of all the more value because he did not aim at this. But, in our opinion, the best apologetic in the book is the author's life—its beauty, its logic, its strong scientific enthusiasm, constantly rekindled at the fire of a religious mysticism whose sincerity could be doubted by no one.

That said, we must come to the best-founded attacks that have been made on the book.

### FATHER BOSIO

The great Roman Catholic review, *La Civiltà Cattolica* (17 December 1955), published an important article, under the signature of Father G. P. Bosio, S.J.; this was reprinted in the *Osservatore Romano* of 23 December, and then translated into French in *Documentation catholique* (22 January 1956). Informed people tell us that the Holy Father read the *Civiltà* article in proof before publication. In any case the judgement of this review is something of weight, though it carries no obligation upon Christians' conscience, except in so far as it is based on recognized and established dogma.

We must therefore pay careful attention, and respect, to this article of the venerable Father Bosio, who is himself known as reviewer of scientific questions in the Roman organ.

He begins by paying respect, as we all do, to Père Teilhard's scientific qualifications. 'There is no doubt', he concludes, 'that Père Teilhard de Chardin was a great scientist.' But besides a scientist he was also a bold, and often controversial 'speculator'. All through his life he had issued more or less secret and mysterious writings which had given rise to objections or caused astonishment. But in this book, *Le Phénomène humain*, published after his death under the distinguished patronage of an honorary committee among which were some of the greatest names in science, from one end to the other we find the ideas which he had already expressed in his secret writings. We must therefore examine what these ideas are worth.

## EVOLUTION

'The first and basic idea which can be found on every page', writes Father Bosio, '. . . is that of cosmic evolution, in which the transformation of the species, right up to man inclusively, takes its place—and not as arresting that evolution but as giving it a new impetus.' And Father Bosio quotes passages which we have given above. They prove that for Teilhard evolution is more than a hypothesis, more than a system, but rather 'a general condition which all theories, all hypotheses, all systems must fit into and satisfy if they are going to be either *thinkable* or *true*'.

This fearless assertion seems to Father Bosio to be excessive. 'We cannot', he says, 'conceal our perplexity in the presence of such categorical assertions.' According to him the doctrine of evolution remains a hypothesis, whatever Teilhard may say. And he refers not only to the opinion of scientists of great repute, but also to the attitude clearly expressed by Pope Pius XII in the Encyclical *Humani generis*. Is there, then, something in the principle of evolution which is opposed to Christian dogma? The Encyclical *Humani generis* points here to the danger of falling into *monism* and *pantheism*. It is obvious that if evolutionism—without any valid reason from the scientific point of view—is erected into a *monistic* and *pantheistic* explanation of all things, it stands condemned both by common sense and by the Christian faith. But is this danger inevitable? We do not think that the papal Encyclical says so, nor that Père Teilhard's book gives one to think so.

It will be of interest to bring in here, at some length, the testimony of another great scientist, the abbè Henri Breuil, in his talk given on the radio (21 November 1955):

'We both of us think', he said, 'that the principle of Evolution—as Cardinal Mercier also agreed, in a long conversation I had with him at Malines, on March 27th, 1925—is only the scientific method itself applied to everything of every kind that develops within time. It is the only means at our disposal to try to grasp the law of their expansion and succession, whatever may be their ontological basis. Without it all one could do would be to draw up a descriptive catalogue of things without attempting to understand them. "To know that everything real, whatever it is, comes largely from what precedes it, and is itself largely the source of what follows it": we can postulate this without making any inferences outside the order of tangible things, about the spiritual principle which orders this succession of events in developing stages. *This process is not a hypothesis, but the definition of the method.*'

That was, we believe, fundamentally what Teilhard thought. He never had the least tendency to use Evolution in order to eliminate the power of the Creator. On the contrary, to him and men of his way of thinking, Evolution demands the continuous action of creative Wisdom more imperiously than does Fixity (of species), for we are clearly concerned with an Evolution which has a purpose, a *directed* Evolution, an Evolution which itself suggests that once it has reached its summit, which is Man, it has nothing more to do but to stop and leave Man himself the task of following it through in the order of reflective consciousness. To the abbé Breuil evolution is a fact of daily experience.

'Anybody can observe the elementary fact of the metamorphosis of insects', he said on the radio. '. . . Evolution can be verified in every being and every reality, including science itself. It is therefore rational to suppose that it has always been the same in the past and that it will always be the same under our very noses as we advance into the future. This is the unshakable principle on which Père Teilhard based his outlook on things, and no scientist can do without it, either in his all-over interpretation, or in the most restricted field of his research, whatever may be his education and temperament, and even if he dresses it up in some other terminology.'

As we read these lines we wonder whether there is not simply a misunderstanding between Father Bosio and the abbé Breuil or Père Teilhard. We are among those who believe that the idea of evolution, understood as a method of exposition and without prejudice to its ontological value, has become unavoidable in all domains of thought. But before going further we would like to recall certain texts of St. Augustine which seem entirely favourable to the idea of evolution, such as Teilhard understands it. They are to be found in his work *De Genesi ad litteram* ('Literal Commentary on Genesis'). Augustine starts by observing that if God, in Genesis, took six days to create things, in Ecclesiastes xviii. 1, it is said 'The Eternal has created all things together.' A little further on Augustine writes: 'There are those who think that God merely made the world, and that all the rest was done by the world itself, following His orders and instructions, but God Himself doing no more. But that runs counter to what Christ said: "My Father worketh always . . ." (John v. 17). So we must believe and try to understand that if His "operation" were to disappear from things, they would be annihilated.'

But having said that, Augustine reckons that God put an evolutionary power into things. This is how he expressed the thought: 'Just as in the seed all the elements which in the process of time must appear in the tree, are already invisibly together in the seed: so one must consider the world, once God has created all things at once, as possessing in embryo all that is going to appear later when its moment has come.' And Augustine adds that this is not only true of the sky, the sun, the moon and the stars, but also of the earth and the seas, which seem subject to less regular motions; so that, he says, God has produced *potentialiter et causaliter* (in their potential and causative form) all that which the earth and the waters would produce in their season.'[1]

There is therefore certainly a Christian manner of understanding evolution, and we are sure that this is what Teilhard followed.

## UNITY OF THE WORLD

Next Father Bosio criticizes the special doctrine of Teilhard's in *Le Phénomène humain* which we have, like everyone else, called *panpsychism*, on which he bases the fundamental unity of the world. Here again it seems that Father Bosio above all regrets that Teilhard does not make the slightest allusion to creative intervention. This silence on his part does not mean at all that he denies creation. On the contrary, directed evolution as he understands it demands creation more imperiously than fixity does. An evolution such as he describes must have had a beginning and will have an end. So it demands a Creator much more than an immobile world which could in theory have always been such as it is. We believe therefore that if Teilhard does not speak or even allude to 'an act of the divine Creator', 'for the creation of those very first elementary corpuscles' from which everything else derives by evolution, it is only because, addressing his colleagues, agnostic scientists, he would not or could not lead them except by degrees to his conviction that all is dependent on the 'Omega point', in such a way that 'Omega' is equally, and more emphatically, 'the Alpha point'.

Here again it is only a question of a method of exposition, and it is not here that we should see the questionable part of his general theory; that we should find rather, with Bosio indeed, in his 'panpsychism'. We find it difficult to take literally that the whole universe contains right from the first 'a certain degree of life, and therefore a certain degree of consciousness'; that the Earth, broken off and separated from the

[1] These passages, and those which follow them, are to be found in Migne. *Patr. Lat.*, I. 34, col. 333–8.

Sun, took with it its own portion of life and consciousness. It is difficult to picture what the 'consciousness' of a neutron, of an electron, even at an 'infinitesimal' degree, might be like. The abbé Breuil, in his radio talk already mentioned, tried to explain it in this way: 'In all things there is *an inward side*, which is psychic, linked no doubt to determined chemical and organic elements, but not homogeneous with them. Our own experience gives us the only direct knowledge of this. At the root of our consciousness which endures, plays, fears, hopes, dreams, thinks, approves, rejects, etc., whatever may be the subject of these experiences, this "something or other", although connected with our nervous system, is still distinct from it. Now we are not free to imagine another being that would not be constructed to some degree (whether by addition or subtraction) on another model: anthropomorphism then is necessary and unavoidable, when we try to interpret the elements of the non-I, of which only the exterior is accessible to us; and experiments will never directly show us anything other than its outside, its behaviour.'

The abbé Breuil then seems to approve of Teilhard's extrapolations, pushed as far as the atom. Indeed, he approves of them so thoroughly that after the lines quoted above, he adds: 'Such is Teilhard's method, and such must be the method of every scientist and thinker, and no one can object to it.' In spite of this, however, we are not convinced, and we still cannot see the necessity, nor even the possibility of an 'Inside' of things, at the level of 'things', that is to say, outside of life. However, this is a problem to be thrashed out between scientists or philosophers, in which the Christian faith is not involved. We think it one of those questions of which St. Augustine said: *In dubiis libertas.*[1]

We do not think that even the most ardent admirers of Teilhard will feel themselves bound to follow him all the way in his zeal for 'the fundamental unity of the world'. We believe that this unity is sufficiently manifested in the dependence which the Creator has established between the higher and lower stages of His work. Life can only be realized on top of a foundation of inanimate matter. Thought itself, in man (it is not the same in angels), needs this foundation of life for its appearance. There is then a continuity, willed by the great 'Demiurge' which has ordained the whole unfolding of evolution, between all the degrees of this evolution. The unity of the world, then, is a unity of plan, though it is not necessarily a unity of structure, consisting genuinely at all stages of a *Within* and a *Without* of things, like a body and soul in our case.

[1] 'Freedom in doubtful matters'.

## THE APPEARANCE OF MAN

In the rest of his article Father Bosio is just as hard on the sketch of Evolution, such as Teilhard describes it, in its culmination in man and its continuation by man and in man. After having briefly summarized Teilhard's views, as we already know them, he declares: 'It is hardly necessary to point out that it is the same highly complex phenomena of past, present and future sociology that can be put up against Teilhard's attempted explanation, which is too simple and equivocal in that the author turns possible analogies into principles of identity.'

What makes Father Bosio so severe is that he finds that Teilhard, although leaving place—under 'the phenomenal veil' of evolution leading to man—for any 'special intervention' you like to explain the soul, is here scarcely making any but a 'verbal concession'. True, Teilhard admits that there is a 'leap' which suddenly 'transformed' the subject undergoing evolution. But that is not enough for Father Bosio, who writes: 'These lines and other similar passages certainly do not suggest to the reader the idea of the direct creation of the human soul, for one is still left unable to decide whether, for the whole system, the author makes any clear distinction between matter and mind.'

This is serious. The readers of *Le Phénomène humain* must guard against an inaccurate interpretation here. We have not the slightest doubt of Teilhard's complete orthodoxy on this particular point: but it may be that his language was not sufficiently explicit, and Father Bosio's objections show that the danger of being misunderstood was real enough.

On the other hand Father Bosio regrets that Teilhard speaks 'with an absolute assurance, which is foreign to the rigour of science' about 'the origin of man's body'. To be sure, absolutely sure from the scientific point of view, about the animal origin of the human body, we need proofs and not merely indications. And Father Bosio once more recalls the Encyclical *Humani generis,* which urges prudence in this realm. However, we must believe that naturalists, geneticists, prehistorians, increasingly regard this question as finally settled. Actually it cannot be so, by very reason of the rule which Teilhard pointed to, of the 'disappearance of the stems'. A mutation leaves no trace of its passage once it has produced its results. The point of junction between the new phylum and the old is inaccessible to our experience. We are, and we shall perhaps always be, unable to say whether *Sinanthropus* was already a man, whether it gave birth to an intermediate form on the way to man, or whether man was born starting from quite another stock. However it does not seem very probable that we shall ever return to the idea, accepted by our forebears in the name of the Bible, of the direct formation of man, in his body and soul, by the Creator, starting from clay or a lump of mud.

### MONOGENISM

Father Bosio in his criticism of Père Teilhard, also insists on the question of monogenism. He objects to a phrase in the book which we must quote here, so that we can examine it closely and find its real meaning: '*From the point of view of Science* then, which from a distance only covers collectivities, the "first man" is and can only be a crowd; and his youth is made up of thousands and thousands of years.' (pp. 205–6.)

What does this passage mean? Not that, for science, men appeared at the same time all over the world, from numerous couples and not from a single couple only; but that since the *stem* has disappeared here as elsewhere, science cannot know anything of what happened. When it does find man in the past, he has no doubt already been there for a long time, and it can only find him as a crowd. Chellean man, for instance, which comes from France, is roughly contemporary with *Sinanthropus* of China or *Pithecanthropus* of Java. What proves that this is Teilhard's meaning is his footnote (p. 206): 'That is why the problem of *monogenism* . . . seems by its very nature to escape science as such.' So from a scientific point of view Teilhard is neither monogenist nor polygenist. He is within his rights here. Father Bosio's objections to him on this point do not, then, seem well founded. We always come back to the same thing: one must not ask Père Teilhard to give us something that did not enter into his plan. And we think the same principle must be applied to two other criticisms of Father Bosio's. One relates to the 'Omega point', on which Father Bosio thinks that though the doctrinal substance of it may be safeguarded, it is at least 'minimized'. We do not agree. If one considers the public to which Teilhard's book was addressed, what he says about the 'Omega point' is incontestably a great victory over the agnosticism which he so often came up against among the prehistorians and naturalists he mixed with.

The second point Father Bosio touches on, in concluding, concerns the problem of evil. Bosio thinks that the *supernatural* character of Redemption and Revelation was not sufficiently emphasized by Teilhard. But more serious, he thought, was the fact that the problem of moral evil seemed to be 'misrepresented and misunderstood'. Father Bosio says, 'Everything seems to be reduced to the *evil of* the *disorder* due to *failure*', because of 'the play of large numbers in a multitude which is gradually getting organized; to the *evil of decomposition*, that is of sickness and death; to the evil of *solitude* and of *anguish*, and to the evil of *growth*, that is to say of progress which demands effort and hard work.' But Père Teilhard appears to forget evil *par excellence*, namely *sin*, the revolt of man against God under the impulse of Satan. The great drama of human history, in so much as it implies an immensity of moral disorder, overcome and conquered by a still greater immensity of pity and love in the Incarnation and Redemption, ought to have been faced with more clarity and force, in Teilhard's general vision of things: and ought to have been seen as one of the essential 'dimensions' of our human Phenomenon. We think that this is the most serious and the best-established objection to Teilhard's book from the doctrinal point of view. At a time like ours, when unfortunately the idea and the very word *sin* seem to be disappearing, we should dearly have liked to see a mind as powerful as Teilhard's take up a firm position on this and range himself with his immortal compatriot, Blaise Pascal.

## THE JUDGEMENT OF LOUIS COGNET

The reaction we have just voiced can be found in the vigorous little book by the abbé Louis Cognet, called *Père Teilhard de Chardin and Contemporary Thought*, which appeared in 1952. At the end of an always courteous and temperate discussion, the author of this book points, with a clarity and firmness that leaves nothing to be desired, to Père Teilhard's doctrinal inadequacies. Louis Cognet disclaims, as we do, any attempt to challenge Teilhard the palaeontological specialist. In this realm the judgement must be left to his equals. But as *thinker* he belongs to us. That is the part of him which allows us to measure him, to weigh him up in some sense. And to do so we must put ourselves at the point from which he started.

So, along with Louis Cognet, we shall begin by unreservedly praising him for his major ambition and his courage.

## THE VAST SCOPE OF TEILHARD'S PROJECT

What did Teilhard really want to do? Louis Cognet, like we ourselves, reckons that his basic preoccupations were 'apologetic'. That is because he saw better than anyone else, and without any illusions, the greater danger which threatens us today: 'A world which is being built without God, an ontology in which God has no possible place any more.' He lived 'passionately with his own time'. He saw the new, and the partly devastating, light brought by modern science to our vision of the world. Can we ignore the problems posed for our faith by this universe which grows larger every day through contemporary astronomy and radio-astronomy, this universe whose evolutionary stages we are beginning to be able to plot, to calculate its extension in Time, to trace its march through the centuries: can we ignore these problems simply by closing our eyes, or ought we not, on the contrary, to face these problems with that faith which is more dear to us than life itself and without which the *zest for life* would swiftly disappear from the world? Teilhard de Chardin resolutely adopted the second alternative. And Louis Cognet praises him for it without hesitation. And he sums up his objective thus: 'He (Teilhard) wanted to show that the religion in which he believed was in no way outstripped or destroyed by the new hopes engendered by science. "A religion which is judged inferior to our human ideal is a lost religion", he exclaimed. Precisely because he penetrated to the very bottom of this human ideal, he felt he had the right to affirm that in face of it Christianity still preserved all its value, even that it could integrate this human ideal and magnify it to unforeseen limits.'[1]

We can certainly say that all his life Teilhard lived to supply the proof to his scientific colleagues of this total convergence of the Universe through Jesus Christ to God. All his writings, of which *Le Phénomène humain* is only the crown, tended towards this great end. And Louis Cognet[2] admits the grandeur of this aim: 'For the first time', he writes, 'the Christian problem in all its wide scope is posed here in face of the most modern scientific data, of the most recent acquisitions of the human mind. Here is an admirable attempt at re-thinking our great Christian truths within the framework of contemporary thought. Whatever may be our later judgements, we must first salute this courageous and ambitious attempt, before which we cannot remain

[1] Cognet, op. cit., p. 26. [2] Ibid., p. 57.

indifferent. Even if we have to indicate blocks at many points, it is certain that this synthesis points the road and opens the way for future explorers.'

May we be allowed to make these lines our own: and they should never be forgotten. Whatever may finally be thought of Père Teilhard's work, there is one merit we cannot refuse him, that of having seen the task that needed to be done, that must be done at all costs, and that he was the first bravely and steadily to tackle.

## INADEQUACIES

Having said this, the abbé Cognet points clearly, as we have done, to the inadequacies of Teilhard's bold synthesis. An inadequacy in his distinction between science and hypothesis; an abuse of private hypotheses which are far from being inevitable; an inadequacy in showing the junctures between science and faith on the one hand, and the transcendence of faith over science on the other. It is clear, for instance, that Teilhard might have stuck more closely to the biblical data, or entered much more deeply into an analysis of the human tragedy, while still showing that this tragedy goes far beyond anything that pure science is capable of meeting.

'Teilhard was so preoccupied with safeguarding the unilinear and continuous character of evolution', says Louis Cognet, 'that he hasn't always pointed in his system to the "toothing-stones" to which the Christian data can be built in. I believe that these toothing-stones exist, but they are not very obvious to the majority of readers, and Père Teilhard should have indicated them. . . . Some of his pages leave a strong impression that the history of the world is a coherent unrolling, single and continuous, strictly immanent, and one into which no transcendence could be introduced. It is understandable, then, that many of his articles, even the purely scientific ones, provoked uneasiness in many of his readers.' (p. 92.)

Admittedly in the final version of his *Phénomène humain* Teilhard at two or three points added footnotes which opened the way for transcendence. But these notes rather give the impression of corrections, such as painters of frescoes use, and of making no difference to the final vision of things in his own mind.

Louis Cognet points cogently to the philosophical imprecision of Teilhard's vocabulary. He uses the words soul, spirit, consciousness, thought, without the necessary distinctions. He has not stressed sufficiently 'man's transcendence' in relation to the rest of creation. Yet man's immortal soul is something which surpasses all the rest of the created universe. One single soul is of more *value* than all the galaxies put together. Teilhard knew that, or rather believed it, no doubt. He might have said so in some way or other. On the contrary, his *panpsychism*, which we have found to be so arbitrary, tends rather to undervalue the *spirit*. And by seeing sublimity everywhere, he seems to be prevented from seeing it anywhere.

But if he does not give the transcendence of man sufficient prominence, it can be said that the same is true of divine transcendence. Louis Cognet objects to the fact that he 'dismisses as vulgar opinions the three ideas: that God could absolutely either create or not create; that if He did create, He could do so with or without an Incarnation; and that if He was to be Incarnate, He could have been so with or without suffering.' (p. 129.) But these three opinions are well supported in theology. Creation was not necessary to God. If He did create, He was not obliged (whatever Scotus may have said) to become Incarnate. If He became Incarnate, He was not bound to go so far as to the bleeding sacrifice of His Cross. In all this Teilhard forgets the infinite *gratuity* of the divine love. Creation was gratuitous. The Incarnation was the pure fruit of a love that is without constraint: 'God so loved the world . . .' etc., said St. John. And the Cross was but the final and absolutely gratuitous summit of love. Teilhard seems on all these points to have expressed inadmissible ideas; but in any case he removed them from the version of *Le Phénomène humain* which we have. Louis Cognet quotes passages belonging to his semi-clandestine publications, which no healthy theology could ever accept.

But what Louis Cognet makes quite clear is that this conception of the Incarnation and Redemption in Teilhard is essentially bound up with the glaring inadequacy of his theory of evil. Thus we come back to the point that has already been touched on above.

'The traditional notion of Redemption', writes Cognet (p. 131), 'is linked with the idea of a guilt to be wiped out, a ransom to be made, a slavery to be destroyed. But in Père Teilhard de Chardin's thought, the kingdom of darkness does not seem to have any genuine reality: the idea of man fallen and in bondage to the devil does not seem to be evident to him. In his system, evil is confused with the different natural inertias towards which man and the world lurch in their advance into the future.'

That is why he talks readily of the Incarnation but less readily of the Redemption. He often returns to the mystery of the Cross, but he no longer gives it its full meaning. There is a certain aroma of pelagianism in Teilhard's system. Christ for him, as for Pelagius, is first and above all 'a sort of universal centre of psychic convergence'. Christ is a guide, a model, a trainer. It is not made sufficiently clear that He is above all the Saviour, the Source of grace, the only Mediator between God and Man.

Louis Cognet feels himself bound to conclude: 'Père Teilhard has not managed to include in his synthesis either the contingent element, sin, or the supernatural element, grace. Inevitably his theology of the divine action suffers for it.' (p. 146.)

At the end of his thorough and penetrating examination, Louis Cognet declares that one can allow hardly any one of the components of Teilhard's synthesis just as they stand. But he insists on saying once more that 'it is, however, a courageous attempt to think out the Christian problems again within the framework of contemporary mentality'. True, it will need much more meditation, many more attempts in order to bring the work he undertook to that point of maturity which we should all like to see. Something is happening which is analogous to the revolution of St. Thomas Aquinas assimilating Aristotelianism and incorporating it, not as it stood, but in its valid elements, into the heart of Christian doctrine. Teilhard wanted to be the Thomas Aquinas of our time. We cannot say that he has managed to rise to that ambitious height. 'In any case,' we shall join Louis Cognet in saying, 'none of these reservations can diminish his merit as an initiator.' We are not among those, then, who regret the publication of his book. It will remain among us, at the very least, as a sort of 'miscellany of themes to be pondered'. The problems are there. He saw them. It remains to resolve them.

# CHAPTER NINE

# Sympathetic Voices

## A CHANGE OF PERSPECTIVE?

HAVING given a whole chapter to criticisms of Teilhard's doctrine, we now give another, of equal length, to the intellectual manifestations of sympathy which have been shown to this doctrine. But it must not be thought that there is a radical opposition between these two consecutive chapters. We have seen, in fact, that even those who, like Father Bosio and Louis Cognet—to whom we could have added P. Villain, editor of *Etudes*—have felt bound to raise serious objections, have not hesitated also to give well-merited praise. However with them the final effect comes out as largely *negative*, in the sense that the objections seem to outweigh the praise. With those whom we are now going to quote, on the other hand—and we cannot quote them all—the final effect will be clearly *positive*, in the sense that although they modify their admiring approval with reservations very much like those we have already noted, these reservations are only on a lower level. When you add it up, there is not, perhaps, a very great distance between the two positions, but only, to put it thus, a change of perspective. These want Teilhard to be seen simply as a rugged pioneer, a precursor of genius, who 'must be forgiven much, for he loved much'.

## R.P. N. M. WILDIERS, O.F.M.

In the front rank of these warm admirers of Teilhard we shall place the philosopher Claude Tresmontant on the one hand, and the Doctor of Theology from Louvain, N. M. Wildiers, on the other. We shall take them in turn.

N. M. Wildiers is not only the one who stood guarantee for the publication of *Le Phénomène humain* by writing and signing the Foreword. He is also the author of a study of fourteen full pages, published in *La Table Ronde* (June 1955), entitled 'The Fundamental Experience of Père Teilhard de Chardin'. This experience, according to him, was the necessity for a decisive explanation, and above all for a loyal and complete confrontation between the natural sciences and Christianity. Teilhard had the uncommon position of being at once a thorough *believer*, a priest deeply attached to his priesthood, a religious voluntarily devoted to God by indissoluble vows, and a *scientist* of the front rank. Up till his time men were more or less content to leave catholicism and the natural sciences to live apart as two distinct worlds which had almost nothing to say to each other. But Teilhard understood that this attitude is no longer possible. History sweeps us on. 'We must recognize the truth', said Teilhard in 'The Present Crisis' (*Etudes*, October 1937), 'that humanity has just entered what is probably the greatest period of transformation it has ever known. The basis of the evil we are suffering from now is to be found at the crucial point of terrestrial thought. Something is happening in the structure of human consciousness. It is another species of life that is just beginning.'

Many people do not suspect this, or take no notice of it. A little later, again in *Etudes* (March 1939), Teilhard repeated it, showing that 'scientific research has grown out of its child's play; it has become the serious, central, and vital operation of adult man'. Science is not simply the fruit of the desire for knowledge or for extending man's powers. It is acquiring cosmic powers. It aspires to take charge of humanity and the future of the World. Unhappily contemporary science, 'instead of attaching the advance of things to a higher pole of the spirit . . . imagines it as being supported and limited by the elementary powers of the Multiple. It has projected the centre of the World down towards the bottom. Its mystique has strayed into the worship of matter.'

This is the point at which a shift is urgently necessary. Research must be given a sense of the sacred. So Teilhard came to this conviction which was to inspire all his activity and all his writings, that 'There is no future for humanity without science. But no more science will be possible without some religion to inspire it.' And so he saw it as indispensable that there should be a remedy for the divorce introduced between scientific progress and Christianity. The task was colossal. Teilhard wanted to do nothing other than that, in his own domain and by virtue of the high authority which his name had acquired through his scientific work. And to do so, he aimed to tear Christian theology away from its ancient static vision of things, by showing that the law recognized by science, namely universal evolution, was in no way opposed to faith.

In his essay on *The Heart of the Matter*, which belongs to 1950, Teilhard himself described his inner evolution. 'He emphasizes', says N. M. Wildiers, 'that his ideas are the result of a slow and natural process of growth, and that his great scientific experience, as well as his profound religious feeling, provided the ideal field for this growth.'

What he saw so clearly is that Man is not an accident, an 'irregularity', an insignificant phenomenon, at the heart of nature, but on the contrary, an essential aspect of the Cosmos. So he says, in his essay on 'The Heart of Matter': 'Zoologically and psychologically speaking, Man, finally seen in the cosmic integrity of his trajectory, is only at an embryonic stage of it, beyond which we can already see in outline a large fringe of the Ultra-Human.'

But Teilhard, says Wildiers, affirms stoutly that the advance forward cannot be made without a faith, and that this faith can only be Christianity. 'The essence of Christianity', he wrote in *Social Heredity and Education*, 'is nothing more nor less than the belief in the unification of the world in God through the Incarnation.'

And from then on, says Wildiers, Teilhard de Chardin 'never ceased to talk about this harmony between the *comsic sense* and the *Christian sense*: on the very eve of his death, in an essay "Le Christique", he praised its marvellous beauty. He entered into eternity with this vision before his eyes.'

And Wildiers' conclusion is that, faced by such vast and such sound observations, there are better things to do than merely in a niggly way to pick on the gaps or the inadequacies, as we pick out spots on the sun. For him, as we have said, the balance sheet of Teilhard's action is largely *positive*: 'Teilhard de Chardin's experience', he writes, 'is an event of exceptional value for our era.' And why? Because 'No one has realized better than he the depth and the acuteness of the conflict between traditional theology and the new vision of the world', and 'No one too has searched for the solution with more fervour.' Yes, admittedly his work is unfinished, his system is disputable in places, but he has opened the way. He has planted the first landmarks. He has exercised an influence which is 'very rare'. 'He deserves', says Wildiers—and here we agree—'to be called in every sense of the word, a pioneer and a trail-blazer.'

To conclude: 'Teilhard de Chardin's work must be pursued. We must ponder his theses in a critical manner, and re-think his arguments. Meanwhile we shall remember with gratitude the man who has so honestly and so completely done full justice both to the scientific conceptions of our era and to the religious aspirations of the human soul.'

## CLAUDE TRESMONTANT'S POINT OF VIEW

This attitude of N. M. Wildiers is largely that of Claude Tresmontant. But the latter has pursued his examination of Teilhard's thought much further. He has tried to act in the full sense of the word, as a guide through this thought. He has undertaken to help the general public to understand the depth and the relevance of his doctrine. He published a short book entitled *Introduction à la Pensée de Teilhard de Chardin* ('Introduction to the Thought of Teilhard de Chardin') (Éditions du Seuil, 1956). There he expounds: (1) Teilhard's Vision of the World; (2) Teilhard's ideas on Christ, on spirituality, on creation, and the problem of evil. In the first part we find exactly Teilhard's system, as we have expounded it ourselves, in an analysis of *Le Phénomène humain*. There is no point in again going over this analysis. But what is worth recording in Tresmontant is his observations on the objections made against his hero—who is our hero too.

What above all Tresmontant has seen—and rightly seen—is that Teilhard's views are in the direct line of biblical teaching. Did Teilhard know it? It does not appear that he had any very advanced scriptural knowledge. But he must have known certain texts of St. Paul and St. John, about which Claude Tresmontant has written as follows (*La Revue Nouvelle*, 15 June 1955): 'To understand Teilhard de Chardin's thought, we must put ourselves in the Pauline perspective of the Epistles of the Captivity (i.e. Colossians, Ephesians, Philippians). Christ the Origin of all creation; the Christ in whom, by whom and for whom all things in heaven and earth were created; the Christ to whom all Creation yearns and tends, for He is the Head of the Body which is the Church, and in Him all things consist; He is the coping-stone, and the corner-stone of the whole Building; Christ the beginning and the end of God's work, the Alpha and the Omega, *Christos pantokrator* (Christ the All-Ruler).'

And again, 'Teilhard's fundamental intention seems to have been to discern in creation itself as it appears to us today through Science, the work of the Word who, says St. John, *worketh hitherto*; and St. Paul says that the whole of creation groans and travails in pain together until now. Creation waits impatiently till humanity has arrived at "a full-grown man", to the fullness of Christ, to receive its supernatural inheritance, participation in the life of God in Christ and with Christ.'

We agree with Tresmontant that these are neglected aspects of St.

Paul and St. John, and that Teilhard's writings should help to make them rightly better known; we only regret that Teilhard himself did not make a profounder use of them. 'Teilhard was very little skilled in the Bible,' admits Tresmontant (*Introduction*, p. 97), 'but the correspondence of the two is all the more striking; Teilhard off his own bat rediscovered the principles of a mysticism of a biblical type.'

Where we should be less positive than Tresmontant is when he says that 'Teilhard's spirituality can be defined as a masterly attempt to free Christian spirituality and mysticism from the remnants of Manicheanism which still unconsciously burdened them. . . .' Teilhard's imperturbable optimism stood constantly aside from the no less biblical affirmations according to which Satan is and remains 'the Prince of this World', and according to which we have to contend not merely 'against flesh and blood, but against principalities and powers, against the rulers of the darkness of this world, against spiritual wickedness in high places'. (Eph. vi. 12.) Surely it is not in this that Tresmontant finds 'remnants of Manicheanism'. But we are not so sure as he is that Teilhard has given the place it deserves to this Pauline—and also evangelical—conception of the dominion of Satan. It is still the notion of sin that seems defective in him. He had fine views on many points, then, but he did not manage to encompass the human drama in all its tragic beauty. His outlook on the Cosmos was too complacent. Something was missing. Tresmontant himself admits as much when, among so many well-deserved encomia which he addresses to his hero, he writes, 'What is tragic in Teilhard's destiny is that he was never able to place and define, in relation to his own and his circle's outlook, this discovery he made of a Christianity which is simply basic Christianity—that of holy Scripture, of the Fathers and of the most unvarying tradition of the Church. This is where one most regrets that Teilhard did not have a better theological training in biblical and patristic studies.' (Op. cit., p. 100.)

We shall not perhaps always agree with Tresmontant in the points where he thinks Teilhard was right as against the spirituality he had been brought up in. But we touch on one of the most contentious theories of Teilhard's when, with Tresmontant, we find him saying that creation is not 'gratuitous' on God's part. We have already said that Teilhard's error on this point is certain and obvious. On this Tresmontant writes: 'To avoid the Charybdis of a Universe created in a purely contingent and arbitrary manner, Teilhard falls into the Scylla of a well-known mythology: God completes Himself by creating the World, God engages in a struggle with the Multiple (the ancient

"Chaos") and ends up richer and appeased: this is an old gnostic idea which can be found in Boehme, Hegel and Schelling. . . .'

Clearly this is one of the most seriously defective points in Teilhard's theory. And yet he could so easily have avoided both Charybdis and Scylla. How? Simply by remembering St. John's definition of God, a definition which in any case fits in so well with all Teilhard's thought: *God is love!* No, Creation was not necessary for God to fulfil Himself. But nor is it for that reason useless and insignificant. It is the *chef-d'œuvre* of an infinite Love, on condition that we see it crowned by the Incarnation of the Word, and we understand in all its depth the text already quoted, 'God so loved the world that he gave his only-begotten Son. . . .' (John iii. 16.)

Finally we should have difficulty in following Claude Tresmontant in the easy acquittal he gives Père Teilhard for his ideas about *evil, sin, redemption* and the sense of suffering. Teilhard does not seem to admit that God could 'create from nothing a World without pain, without flaws, without risks, without "breaks"'. According to him, Evil was an inevitable result of creation itself. Here again, what we think he lacked was a profound enough view of love. God creates out of love because essentially He is Love. He creates to be loved. Creation includes, for its justification, the appearance of beings capable of knowing and loving. But love demands freedom, and freedom is choice, and so the power of giving or refusing oneself, the power of conforming to the divine will in love, or of rebelling against the divine will by an unlawful use of this same freedom. Evil appears as a *risk*, but in no way as a necessity. So we shall not readily allow the idea which Tresmontant calls 'dear to Teilhard' according to which 'suffering is above all the consequence and the cost of the labour of development'. 'It is', writes Tresmontant, 'the suffering of a World which travails in pain and, as St. Paul says, groans together, waiting till humanity shall have come to the perfect stature of Christ.'

Finally, the explanation that Teilhard gives both of the Incarnation and the Redemption, and that Tresmontant seems to support unreservedly, is hardly acceptable to us. Here in fact is the explanation: 'Redemption on these conditions does not come as a repairing of some accident that has occurred to the creative plan of God. The Incarnation and Redemption are integral parts of the creative design of God: the world was created in the Word, and the Word was incarnate to bring creation to its completion. In incarnating Himself, the Word took on the "sin of the world", and the Cross manifests this inevitable law: creation is accomplished through failure and pain. Christ, through the Cross, assumes the law of all creation. Creation, Incarnation, Redemption are in fact inseparable.'

We would say that we find all this picture of the world false, or if not false, at least vague, wavering, uncertain. We should have liked to see Claude Tresmontant saying so distinctly. And we have difficulty in subscribing to his judgement when he concludes with: 'Teilhard is a Scotist.' Scotist, indeed! He had a perfect right to be, of course, but we are not so sure that Scotus would have approved of his doctrine of Creation, encompassing Incarnation and Redemption—for this simple reason, that Scotus did not admit the necessity of creation, as Teilhard does, nor the necessary connection between creation and sin on one side, and suffering on the other. Some distinctions would have to have been made here. However Tresmontant insists on it, going on: 'To a juridical conception of Redemption, Teilhard prefers a conception of Redemption which he has got from the Greek Fathers and the great Franciscan tradition.'

Is this certain? We doubt it. The initial error in fact is still Teilhard's hypothesis of a sort of fulfilling of God in the act of creation, and also that of the necessity of sin at the heart of a created world. We prefer St. Augustine's teaching, when he says that God had rather draw good from evil than suppress the evil. That means that the suppression of evil—which was possible in itself to a God to whom nothing is impossible except that which is a contradiction—would have prevented a greater good, and therefore would have been an evil in itself.

In conclusion, we may grant Tresmontant that Teilhard might have been partly the victim of 'a particular theological education which led him to pose insoluble questions'. (p. 128.) And Tresmontant was also right in distinguishing, with Teilhard as one must do with anybody, 'different literary genres'. He says, quite rightly, 'Let the theologian, in the name of theology, criticize theological writings—that is quite proper. But what is unfair is to ask of Teilhard that he should, in his scientific writing, solve all the theological problems that modern science poses.' But some will want to reply, 'We have no objections to Teilhard's scientific writings, and it is for his peers to judge of their value.' But it is not altogether correct to say that Teilhard in his writings always looked exclusively from the scientific angle. Here and there he seems to claim this, but the text of his work itself is there, to show that he did not always take the strictly scientific point of view.

Tresmontant's book has this fine conclusion: 'Teilhard managed to supplement his love and his adoration with his science.' Under this heading, Teilhard's work deserves something better than party quarrels among his disciples or opponents who limit themselves to partial aspects. It is our desire that the lessons of the past should help us, and that we should learn, as St. Paul asks us to do, 'to prove all things, and hold fast that which is good'. (1 Thess. vi. 21.) And that, we shall say in our turn, is what we should all agree about. Indeed, it is precisely what we have been trying to do here.

## WHAT FRANÇOIS-ALBERT VIALLET HAS TO SAY

So far we have only heard theologians. It is time we should listen to writers who are strangers to theology but speak in the name either of plain philosophy or of science. And first because his witness is important, we shall introduce M. François-Albert Viallet in his book: 'The Personal Universe of Teilhard de Chardin' (*L'Univers personnel de Teilhard de Chardin*, Paris, 1955). Right from the start the author warns us that his aim is to make the person and the thought of Teilhard de Chardin better known, because 'his life and his work, placed under the sign of contradiction, make him a tragically unique case'. The author adds—not without some exaggeration perhaps—that 'rarely has such a personality stirred up so much admiration and love, so much hatred and misunderstanding'. We may admit that Teilhard was little understood, or even largely misunderstood, but we have never ourselves noticed that he became an object of *hatred* to anyone. But let that pass. M. Viallet has undertaken to defend his memory. He is right, and we go with him entirely. We cannot here follow him in the different parts of his study, which is conscientious and attentive, because then we should have to repeat a great part of what we have already said. But we should like to single out certain observations in Viallet's book which are of interest. After having skilfully and intelligently described Teilhard's advance towards his universal vision of things, the author comes to what he calls his *semantic system*. Here again it would be true to say that 'le style c'est l'homme'.

'When', writes Viallet, 'Teilhard de Chardin meets the technical and, to the layman, hermetic style of our contemporary thinkers, who are becoming more and more specialists, he adopts instead a very clear style, and one which has a certain lyrical stress in it. This is at once his strength and his weakness, for a critic might rightly say that he was carried away by some of his terms, that he used picturesque expressions, and therefore sometimes failed in precision.' (p. 75.) He promised us the language of a scientist, and we find ourselves listening to a visionary. Without warning we suddenly get with him 'a mixture of spheres'. He talks, without previous notice, sometimes as a naturalist, sometimes as a poet, sometimes as a prophet, sometimes as a philosopher or even a theologian. M. Viallet is not sure that it is necessary to distinguish between these spheres too closely, and he thinks that the anxiety to do so comes from recent apologetic prudence. But in general we entirely agree with him when he writes: 'What does more to complicate the reading of Teilhard is the notions he invented which are resistant to concrete analysis. We do not mean such terms as "No-osphere", which is a very happy find and is quite unambiguous: but such ill-defined superlatives as "Super-Christ", "Super-Charity", "Trans-Christ", "Supra-Personal", "ultra-monotheism", "super-animated". These expressions have to be taken not in the sense of concrete realities, but rather as pointers towards an idea, for it is illegitimate to handle them like mathematical notions. However, the clarity of some passages suffers from such projections into the absolute whose concrete sense will not be immediately grasped.' (p. 76.)

M. Viallet spoke of people failing to understand Père Teilhard, but he ought not in that case to be surprised at it or to complain of it!

There are many other observations in M. Viallet's book which are worth noting, and several which we could not subscribe to. But we will content ourselves with what he says about a new conception of God according to Teilhard. In *Christology and Evolution* Teilhard says, 'To create, even for the Almighty, must not be understood in the manner of an instantaneous act, but like a process or an act of synthesis.' On which M. Viallet notes as follows: 'All hopes of seeing a "new God" coming to birth are contained in this idea. Traditional Christianity said "God is possible without the World"; materialism put its antithesis: "The World is possible without God"; Teilhard de Chardin, drawing upon the intuition of the mystics, says, "God and the World are not possible without each other."' (pp. 241–2.) Did Teilhard really say this? We find it hard to believe he could. Perhaps he implied it, but if so, with reserves which cancelled out the meaning which is nakedly stated here. What we think is quite certain is that if he did really say it then he would be an indubitable heretic: whereas all his work is a protest against heresy, and he knew enough theology not to fall formally into such a serious error on the absolute transcendence and independence of God with respect to the created. However, we have seen above that Teilhard was not perhaps quite explicit and clear enough on this point. May we briefly recall our own position on this topic. An eternal God, if He could not have existed without the world, must have created from eternity. Christian dogma denies this. But St. Thomas Aquinas declares that theoretically creation *ab aeterno* is not contradictory. He says so for two reasons: first, he will not allow that this eternal creation would be necessary to complete God but that it remains entirely at God's disposal; and second, he conceives of the created world as *fixed* in its condition and not as evolving. The fixed might be eternal, but not the evolving. If evolution had not begun, it would have had an *immeasurable* value. But its continuance under our very eyes proves that it had a beginning. And henceforth it is absurd to say that God could not do without it for His own completion.

But we will not labour the point. Closing Viallet's suggestive book, let us open the *Revue de Paris* (February 1956), to see what a specialist on Evolution, Albert Vandel, has to say.

## ALBERT VANDEL AND TEILHARD

Albert Vandel, who is the author of "Man and Evolution" (*l'Homme et l'Évolution*), does not conceal his admiration and sympathy for Père Teilhard. He speaks of his thought as 'one of the most original of our time'. He emphasizes that 'in the course of his long life of work and research, Père Teilhard had acquired a solid reputation as a geologist and palaeontologist'. 'His colleagues', he says, 'held him in high esteem, and proved it by electing him first as a correspondent (1947) and then as a non-resident member (1950) of the Académie des Sciences.'

But it was not Teilhard's scientific work that most drew universal attention to him and gave rise to so much controversy round his memory. He was more than a scientist: he was a thinker. And A. Vandel adds, as we ourselves have said, that 'He was above all a visionary and a prophet. For this man, professionally concerned with examining the past, was led, by a natural route, from the discovery of the origins of man to the anticipated vision of future humanity.'

However, like so many others, he finds it necessary to manifest a sort of commiseration for Teilhard, because of the hidden persecution which he suffered. He reckons that justice was not shown him—from the Catholic side, obviously—while he was alive, and no doubt also after his death. 'At the very time that Père Teilhard's innovating work was being so systematically suppressed, the critics were left free to say what they liked, and you could see the display-windows of bookshops full of bad pamphlets in which incomprehension vied with stupidity. Many only knew Teilhard's work through these feeble critiques.'

These are hard words. We readily endorse them when we read pages like those of the late A. Franck-Duquesne, called 'From Schweitzer to Teilhard de Chardin' (*De Schweitzer à Teilhard de Chardin*), in *Construire* (October 1955): for in our opinion this criticism strayed beyond the bounds of justice and charity. But after all, Franck-Duquesne was an exception. We cannot say that Teilhard was 'persecuted' for ideas. As we have already shown, he has his partisans who yet feel themselves bound, in soul and conscience, to temper their admiration with numerous reservations; and he has his opponents, who in turn are careful to temper their objections by injecting well-earned praise: so that taken as a whole they are all much closer to each other than they might seem at a first glance. A. Vandel, like M. Viallet and many others, is evidence for what we have just said. For speaking of *Le Phénomène humain* he says, in fact, 'This work, like all Teilhard's, calls forth our admiration as well as our criticism.' And after a rapid summary of Teilhard's vast synthesis, he tells us where the most serious objections have to be made. But we find that it is at the part that Teilhard considered to be most essential that A. Vandel has his reservations. What Teilhard wanted to show, even to demonstrate, was that throughout the immense Evolution which is the law of the Universe, appears an axis, a line of force, a privileged direction, which can be recognized from one end to the other of its progress, from the origins to our own day. If that is not admitted, all 'teilhardism' crumbles. Nothing valid of it remains. But it is *à propos* this fundamental thesis of Teilhard that A. Vandel writes, 'The reader who is faithful to the rigour of science will not fail to object that such a recognition goes beyond our brief. The notion of value does not belong to the realm of science, and it is regrettable to introduce it here.' However, Vandel admits at once that 'the objection does not affect Teilhard's synthesis, since it is a total-view'.

This means, no doubt, that if science is right to limit itself to its own realm, the realm of observation, the thinker who wants to survey the great Whole, above the details of scientific facts, is simply bound to introduce the notion of value. That is what Pascal did; that is what Christian theology has always done. That is above all what Christian mysticism does. Everything is not at one and the same level. To believe in God is to believe in a transcendence, and it is to believe also that it is in relation to God that the scale of values is established.

*In toto*, however, according to Vandel, 'Teilhard's synthesis rests on solid foundations'. One may dispute details, but in the ensemble, 'any natural philosophy which sets out to integrate matter, life and man into one total synthesis, will be led to follow analogous methods'.

Finally, again, in face of the views of the future which Teilhard worked into the summit of his ambitious fresco, A. Vandel writes, 'And yet, Teilhard's prophetic views will not fail to call forth many reservations. Men of science will find them as difficult to accept as integrist Catholics will.' We find the last adjective out of place here. A. Vandel translates Teilhard's thought (we believe inaccurately) thus: 'Teilhard's Omega point reminds us inevitably of Hegel or Renan's God, the God who is not yet but who will be.' If this were true it would be serious, and it would not be necessary to be 'integrist', it would be enough to be just 'Catholic', to condemn Teilhard. However, we agree with A. Vandel in concluding, as he does: 'However that may be, Teilhard's work will be salutary; for it will shatter the quiet of those who hold to tradition, whether scientific or religious. To the one it will show that no mind can today be satisfied with an ancient verbal and introspective experience, and that one cannot any longer ignore the contributions of science. And to the others it will demonstrate the importance—too often neglected—of man in the cosmogenesis: for without him the biological is stripped of all meaning and the world becomes a chaos.'

## NUMEROUS FRIENDS OF TEILHARD

So much has been written about Teilhard in the most varied symposia that it would be easy, but tedious, to multiply texts similar to those we have brought together in this chapter. But we ought not to close without indicating at least the names of the warmest friends and admirers of Teilhard. We shall only have to name those who seem to us the most notable and the most generous. Among them must obviously be included M. Jean Piveteau, an eminent anthropologist[1] and author of a fine study on 'The Organic Conditions for the Human Phenomenon' (*Les conditions organiques du phénomène humain*) in *Anthropologie* (1948). In *La Table Ronde* (June 1955), he gives an account of Teilhard's work, and then pays him this tribute: 'Whether one accepts all his conclusions or whether one refuses to admit them, it cannot be denied that his work marks a turning-point in our palaeontological knowledge and in our vision of the history of the world.'

Claude Cuénot, son of the famous biologist Lucien Cuénot (1886–

[1] palaeontologist? (Tr.)

1951), is also one of those who attaches an exceptional interest to Teilhard's work. He sees him as 'a solitary', as 'the great exile of New York', as a 'resonant echo', one who had the privilege of 'enriching and passing on everything he thought'. And, also writing in *La Table Ronde*, June 1955, he concludes: 'Père Teilhard was a great "awakener" of souls, like Socrates, and his one desire was that everybody should strive to reach his own personal angle, this original point of view which makes every individual irreplaceable. This is perhaps the most valuable thing in the message which the Spirit of Christ charged him to pass on to us, and which, I think, can be summarized in *Wake up and look!*'

And we ought to recall the affection of Max and Simone Bégouën for Teilhard, with whom he kept up such a lively and valuable correspondence. They would certainly have said what the writer and sailor, Henri de Monfreid (*b.* 1879), who was very fond of Père Teilhard, said of him: 'How many unhappy people, discouraged, embittered and disgusted by the blind hostility of the crowd, by injustice and misunderstanding—how many of those who have been disinherited, perverted and lost through distrust of themselves, how many of these have been reassured and rescued by this man who looked at you so directly and who could give life to dead minds as Jesus raised Lazarus from the dead?' This we shall never forget.

And finally among the many studies published on Teilhard, it is pleasant to salute a particularly well-balanced article that appeared in *Ecclesia* (May 1956), written in a spirit of sincere respect and lively admiration for Teilhard, but also with loyalty and frankness in offering criticisms which his work still deserves.

CHAPTER TEN

# The End of a Great Career

WE have paused for a long time, as we had to do, over Teilhard's book, *Le Phénomène humain*, which can be regarded as his 'Testament'. We have called it, as he did, his 'Message', and it is the one work of his which will remain after his numerous scientific essays have been more or less forgotten. It only remains for us to trace briefly the last stages of his splendid career, that of a great traveller, or, as François-Albert Viallet called him, a 'globe-trotter of science'. We know that the war immobilized him at Pekin and that it was there he composed his essential work. During the same period he published in English his *Early Man in China*, of which the abbé Breuil fears that few copies reached Europe; it was dated 1941.

It was the abbé Breuil who made him enthusiastic for the recent palaeontological discoveries in Southern Africa. When he saw Teilhard again in Paris after the war, he found him rather tired from his long experiences during the Second World War. 'I told him', writes the abbé, 'about my experiences down there—in Southern Africa; of the fine stratigraphical studies in the Vaal valley, those of the late lamented Janmart in the diamond mines of Angola and of Dr. Cabu in Katanga-Kasai, the tool-bearing terraces of the banks, rising in narrow tiers from 400 ft. right up to the actual beach, and above all of the extraordinary abundance of discoveries by Dr. R. Dart, Dr. Broom and Dr. J. T. Robinson of the Australopithecinae, at Taungs, and Makapan, right up in the northern Transvaal: of the nearly human characteristics of these anthropoids, to judge by their teeth and their upright posture. I made him promise to come and see all this geological and palaeontological wealth.'

Tired though he already was by this time, Teilhard could not resist such tempting sights. He was more than ever an international expert now. So it was his duty to visit these places, inspect them, 'supervise' them in his own way, and give his opinion of this magnificent chapter in science which had opened in Africa. Alas he had a heart-attack and was ordered a long rest, so that he could not keep the appointment that the abbé Breuil had made for him. And it was after his friend's final departure that he managed to visit Africa himself. He was cordially received and guided by Dr. van Riet-Lowe and also by T. T. Patterson and Dr. Dart. He was able to inspect in detail not only the important collections of fossils in Pretoria and Johannesburg, but also all the sites of the Australopithecinae. 'He recognized', wrote Breuil, 'the character of the Prestellenbosch of the ancient gravels of the Vaal, of which he found *in situ*, for the first time, a fragment in its upper part—usually they are collected from deposits derived from them. Later he learned that Dr. van Riet-Lowe had just discovered others at Makapan, superimposed on beds with Australopithecinae, in position beneath the regional Acheulean level.'

These technical details are valuable to show us how far Teilhard, though he had, as we have seen, become a 'prophet', remained to the end in close contact with pure science.

We have two studies of unequal length of this work on prehistoric Africa, the first of which appeared in *Etudes* (June 1950), and consisted only of five pages, called 'Australopithecinae and the Missing Link' (*Australopithèques et 'chaînon manquant'*). The second appeared in the *Revue des Questions scientifiques* (January 20th 1955), though the date of composition was September 1954, entitled: 'Black Africa and Human Origins' (*L'Afrique noire et les origines humaines*). In these he expressed an opinion which time and the work he inspired will have to test and verify, namely that the answer to the question, 'Where was Man born?' could now at last take a more precise form than it had been able to hitherto.

### THE AFRICAN ORIGIN OF MAN?

In the second of the two articles mentioned he wrote: 'In the course of the last fifty years I have seen this question put by my masters or colleagues: first to Western Europe; then to Asia North of the Himalayas; then to Indonesia. And none of them found an answer. A strange thing, that no one at that time had seemed to have thought about putting the question to Africa, which was apparently regarded as too savage ever to have had anything to do with the beginnings of Humanity.

'But now for some time it has been precisely towards this forgotten continent that everyone has been looking, in Prehistory and in Palaeoanthropology. For it is finally from this part, for different reasons which we shall give, that the answer we are waiting for may well come.' And he goes on to the proofs which he thinks he can provide of an African origin for Man. Strictly speaking they are indications rather than proofs, and he does not forget what he has so often said in the course of his scientific life, about the 'disappearance of the stem'. To catch Man, so to speak 'red-handed', at his origins is impossible now and probably will always be so. It remains however that 'the series of stone industries is more complete—in Africa, in the region of the Great Lakes—and it begins with more "primitive" forms than anywhere else, even than in the *Sinanthropus* beds of Pekin'.

Of course in his view the conclusion that the first Man—a cousin of, but not descended from, the Australopithecinae—was indeed born in Africa, is only a hypothesis, '. . . on which', he wrote, 'tomorrow's discoveries will decide'. But he believed that 'this hypothesis is coherent and fruitful. It holds together.' According to him it would be very tempting and logical to admit a rapid expansion of Man, born in the South of Africa, to the rest of the Earth. 'From the earliest beginnings of the Pleistocene period', he says, 'we are beginning, in the light of recent discoveries, to make out a veritable wave of hominization gathering somewhere in the region of lake Victoria or lake Tanganyika; a wave which progressively spreads out its centrifugal layers from age to age, until, towards the end of the Quaternary, it covers the entire surface of the Earth.'

This was one of the last contributions of Teilhard to the knowledge of our origins. But even in the scientific Memoir whose most important ideas we have just quoted, there was no fear of his forgetting his universal vision of Evolution. For this reason his conclusion should be given in full:

'Indeed it is in Africa, as I said at the beginning, that we are best placed to see the great wave of peoples, of techniques and of ideas, forming, growing, setting off, and then coming back upon itself until it saturates all the habitable earth. And now that the Earth is fully inhabited, and materials are ready and to hand with which, under the irresistible pressure or impetus of planetary forces, the human unity of tomorrow can be built: how ought we to set to, to combine together, in such a way as to give them their fullest value, the diverse ethnic *blocs*, the divers human "isotopes" (the White, the Yellow, the Black . . .), which have been born in the course of time from the double caprice of genes and of the shape of the continents?

'Here is a whole second cycle of Hominization, hardly commenced and now wide open before us!'

Thus he affirms the dominant preoccupation which continued to haunt him during his last years.

### WATCHING A CYCLOTRON

Among Teilhard's last writings there is one which is particularly representative from this point of view. It came out in May 1953, in *Recherches et Débats,* and was called 'Watching a Cyclotron: Reflections on the turning-back upon itself of the Energy of Man' (*En regardant un cyclotron. Réflexions sur le reploiement sur soi de l'Energie humaine*).

Not everybody could draw profound metaphysical considerations from watching a cyclotron. But he immediately became enthusiastic at what he was able to see at the University of Berkeley, California, during the summer of 1952.

'I am not a physicist,' he said, 'and so I shall say nothing here of what my reflections were, in these exalted realms, concerning the explosion or "implosion" of atoms. On the other hand, I think I am an old hand as a student of Life. So in this guise I should like, in the allegorical form of a "double-vision", to express and analyse critically a feeling of spiritual presence and energy which came over me with a shock when for the first time in my life I found myself face to face with one of our modern atom-splitters.'

And what did he see in this mechanical monster which was displayed to him? A 'concentration'. That is, a clear stage in the Evolution of Humanity, prolonging life and even cosmic matter, which have never ceased for a moment to rise from 'concentration' to 'concentration'. '. . . I could not help feeling and seeing,' he says, 'beyond and around this electromagnetic whirlwind, the concentric rush of another and no less formidable radiation: that of Humanity blown by a whirlwind from the four corners of space.' What was needed, he asked himself, to build this cyclotron? What range of efforts was needed to complete it? A *whole range of knowledge and techniques* had to be contributed from all our sciences: mathematics, electronics, chemistry, photography, metallurgy, strength of materials, architecture, etc. And on the other hand a whole spectrum of energies was needed, that is, not only of kilowatt after kilowatt, but of coal, petrol, uranium, and also dollars by the million, that is to say, money—'which it is easy for the virtuous to condemn, but which is still, and indeed every day becomes more and more the life-blood of Humanity'.

And finally, crowning the whole and animating the lot, it was indispensable that in man, in men, should have been found 'a tireless urge to build, drawn from every source of Need and of Desire'.

But it is not only in a cyclotron that this accumulation of physical and moral energies can be tested; the same phenomenon can be seen in every direction—electron microscopes and giant telescopes; space rockets; mechanical brains—on all sides man is sucked in and captivated by his own efforts; and he is finally transformed, in the sense that, Teilhard declares, he is 'ultra-unified' by his operation and the fruits of his operation together.

Teilhard, in his turn, felt as if his thought was carried away by this very movement. 'There was one moment', he says, 'when I noticed that for fifty years we had been present, without being much aware of it, at the birth all over the world of veritable generators (or focusers) of human Energy. Now at this moment I saw clearly that the focusers were focusing upon each other.'

We have just reached an *Age of Research*, for it is no longer a mere curiosity such as man has shown all through the ages, but a 'vortex of Research'. Not a simple agitation in every direction but a real 'Maelstrom', sucking up everything it can encompass towards its central axis. And that means that not only has Evolution, culminating in man, not come to an end, but that it is actually speeding up.

'Let us admit it once for all,' cries Teilhard. 'In us, Men, not only is life not stagnant; not only has it ceased to split up into divergent phyla: on the contrary, it is drawn together by its need for knowledge, and so by its very convergence it has just reached a paroxysm of its characteristic power of advancing Organization and Consciousness, both together and acting on each other, in the Universe: that is to say, its power of interiorizing Matter in order to make it more complex.'

At this moment the cyclotron is no longer there for Teilhard. What he sees, far above himself, is 'The whole No-osphere which, turned back upon itself by the current of Research, forms one enormous cyclone whose proper effect is to produce, in place and instead of nuclear Energy, psychic Energy in an ever more reflective state, that is precisely the Ultra-human state.'

This vision does not make him in the least dizzy: on the contrary it gives him a feeling of calm and joy—'a fundamental calm and joy'.

*Calm*, because the individual feels himself encompassed by an immense, world-wide, logical and irresistible movement. 'Contrary to what existent literature has gone on saying during the past twenty years,' he remarks, 'it is only a general view of Evolution—and not an ever more and more solitary introspection of the individual by the individual—that can, as I have once more been experiencing, save man of the twentieth century from his anxieties in face of Life.'

But along with this great calm, he also experienced joy, the joy of a goal to be reached, the joy of co-operating in the attempt, responding to the twin demands of reflective activity—the need for irreversibility and the need for a total unity.

And then he concludes: 'And that is how the more I tried to prolong, and to discern, in front of me the immense spiral psycho-physical advance in which I found myself engaged by history, the more it seemed to me that what we still call too simply "Research" is charged with, is coloured by, is stirred up by certain forces—Faith, Adoration—up till now regarded as strangers to Science. For the more closely I examined this Research, the more I saw it as compelled by an inner necessity ultimately to concentrate its efforts and its hopes in the direction of some sort of divine focus.'

To comment on this passage would be to dilute and weaken it. It is a passage we should not forget. It is pure Teilhard. *Research* and *Adoration* he believed should essentially come together. Alas, we wonder whether it can happen—though at the same time we whisper: *Utinam!*[1]

## HIS DEATH

Père Teilhard de Chardin was attached in 1951 to the Wenner-Gren Foundation,[2] an institute for anthropological research. It was under this aegis that he made his two trips to South Africa in 1951 and 1953 to organize a scientific network there. His last voyage to France was in 1954. But his centre of action was still New York. And it was there that death came to him. In *Ecclesia* (May 1956), we learn that 'He had always wanted to die on the Day of Resurrection. He said so fifteen days before his death, at a dinner at the French Consulate in New York. On Easter Day, April 10th, 1955, he said his Mass with fervour in the morning, and then went to St. Patrick's Cathedral to attend the pontifical Mass. He lunched with several fathers of the Society of Jesus. In the afternoon he was again at a religious gathering, and then he ended the day with some friends. He was still in an excellent mood. Among other things he delighted the company by saying, "I've never had such a lovely Easter before". Suddenly, as he was going round the room, he fell, like a tree hit by lightning. They gathered round him. He was dead!' His body was interred in the Jesuits' grounds, at Saint-Andrew-on-Hudson, about a hundred miles from New York.

[1] Would it were so!

[2] Formerly the 'Viking' Fund. (Tr.)

## EVALUATION

One cannot leave such a man, after having followed him right through his life, without attempting to assess him, to evaluate him, to assign him a place in history to which henceforward he belongs. But what is to be our basis for so delicate a task? Who can we compare him to, to give him a stature which will not diminish him and yet will not be out of proportion to what he did?

It has been said of him: He was the *Thomas Aquinas of the Twentieth Century*; he wished to reconcile science and faith; he attempted a gigantic work, like Thomas Aquinas in the thirteenth century. Well, no. He did not have the sober style, nor the metaphysical rigour, nor the deep, impeccable and sure knowledge of Christian theology that Thomas Aquinas had. We have heard above one of his admirers telling us that he was a Scotist. But we do not think Scotus was enough of a living figure for us to compare Teilhard with him. The 'Subtle Doctor' does not give us Teilhard's real dimension. With whom then shall we compare him?

Long before Thomas Aquinas and Scotus there was a powerful and lonely genius, a genius who was so bold as to be adventurous and even temerarious, a universal and comprehensive mind, but who was also misunderstood, was attacked and was exiled. All those who know the Fathers will have guessed: Origen. And it is of him that Teilhard instinctively makes us think. The analogies between Origen and Teilhard are, indeed, of several kinds. The first to leap to the attention is that Origen has been a battlefield just like Teilhard. There has been a 'Teilhardist Controversy' just as there was the 'Origenist Controversy' which separated two old friends like Jerome and Rufinus and led to a mortal faction. The Church was disturbed and vexed by origenism as she now is, under our very eyes, by teilhardism. And yet Origen, who was discussed and contested, and even condemned by Councils three centuries after his death, has remained one of the glories of Christian thought. His errors have not prevented us doing him justice and from continuing to hold him in tender regard. We believe the same will be true of Teilhard. He will remain an ornament of Christian thought. In spite of his gaps, his inadequacies, even his errors, he will still be dear to our hearts because of his fine spiritual ambitions, his vast syntheses, his original ideas, and above all—for this above all will survive—his *cosmic sense*. He will have helped finally to lay the ghost of evolutionism, to get us accustomed to it, to see it in a new, fairer and more reassuring light. He will have laboured to enlarge our devotion, our prayer, our spiritual vision, so as to make them not merely planetary but galactic and inter-galactic—that is, genuinely universal. The Christian faith was in essence all those things. But it had somewhat forgotten them. He sought to breathe a new soul into it. And in a large measure he has succeeded.

Finally, the last analogy between Origen and him, though an analogy which we state without being able to applaud it: there was with Teilhard an imperturbable eschatological optimism which is closely allied to the 'final apotheosis' that one finds in Origen, which he substituted for the traditional apocalypses, the 'restoration of all things in God', and in which the demons and Satan himself were finally brought to the centre of light and happiness—to God.

An error of this type has a certain grandeur, without, in our view, ceasing to be an error. It does not lessen the esteem we have for a fine soul. We cannot forget that Père Frédéric-Marie Bergougnioux, O.F.M., Dean of the Faculty of Science at the Institut Catholique of Toulouse and himself a palaeontologist and prehistorian of distinction, when he had to speak about Teilhard to a learned assembly of scientists, did not think he could do better than to speak in glowing terms of 'The priestly heart of Père Teilhard de Chardin'. And his testimony ended with these words:

'May the God of lights open the gates of dazzling Eternity to His servant, Pierre Teilhard de Chardin, priest, professed member of the Society of Jesus!'

Like Father Bergougnioux, we are quite sure that there are two things that can never be taken away from Teilhard de Chardin: to have been a great scientist and a great servant of God.

# BIBLIOGRAPHY


I. Works:

(i) *Le Phénomène humain.* (E.T. *The Phenomenon of Man.*)

(ii) *L'Apparition de l'Homme.*

(iii) *La Vision du Passé.*

(iv) *Le Milieu divin.* (All published by Éditions de Seuil.)

(v) *Le groupe zoologique humain.* (Éditions Albin Michel.)

*Lettres de Voyage* (1923–1939)
and *Nouvelles Lettres de Voyage* (1939–1955). (Grasset.)

II. Works to consult:

(i) Claude Cuénot: *Pierre Teilhard de Chardin, Les Grandes Étapes de son Évolution.* (Plon.)

(ii) Louis Cognet: *Le Père Teilhard de Chardin et la Pensée Contemporaine.* (Flammarion.)

(iii) François-Albert Viallet: *L'Univers personnel de Teilhard de Chardin.* (Amiot-Dumont.)

(iv) Claude Tresmontant: *Introduction à la Pensée de Teilhard de Chardin.* (Éditions du Seuil.)

# INDEX